Charlene Li

THE
ENGAGED
LEADER

A Strategy for Your
Digital Transformation

Wharton
DIGITAL PRESS
Philadelphia

© 2015 by Charlene Li

Published by Wharton Digital Press
The Wharton School
University of Pennsylvania
3620 Locust Walk
2000 Steinberg Hall-Dietrich Hall
Philadelphia, PA 19104
Email: whartondigitalpress@wharton.upenn.edu
Website: http://wdp.wharton.upenn.edu

Web ISBN: 978-1-61363-055-6
Ebook ISBN: 978-1-61363-053-2
Paperback ISBN: 978-1-61363-054-9

For Ben & Katie

*I promised I wouldn't write another book
until you were teenagers.
It was good to wait, to gain perspective, patience.
Thanks for teaching me every day how to keep it real.*

Contents

Introduction

Ginni Rometty has a Twitter account (@GinniRometty), allowing people to message her, but she has yet to post. That's right: The CEO of IBM, the global technology and consulting firm, doesn't tweet, and her presence is minimal in other public social venues such as LinkedIn, Facebook, and Instagram. Does this mean that America's most powerful female CEO doesn't make the grade as an engaged leader? Hardly. She's actually a model leader for a new era.

It's obvious from the partnership IBM formed with Twitter in October 2014 that Rometty grasps fully the potential business value of social data.[1] This followed an equally consequential alliance with Apple to bring the power of mobility into the heart of the enterprise.[2] Rometty doesn't tweet simply because it's not a part of her larger plan. She maintains a laserlike focus on her larger goals, recognizing that there's a big difference between a strategic embrace of the new digital world and superficial symbolism.

Ginni Rometty is exactly the type of digital trailblazer we will examine throughout this book. She understands the power of digital, social, and mobile tools for IBM, and she uses them strategically. For instance, she has overseen the development of what IBM calls a "system of engagement"—including arguably the most liberal social business policy in the corporate world. More fundamentally, she has undertaken a far-reaching transformation of IBM aimed at the historic convergence of big data, cloud computing, mobile, and social—including tens of billions of dollars of both investments and divestitures—to shape IBM for a new era.

As far as her own digital activity is concerned, she is focused on those direct forms of engagement where her personal agency can have the greatest impact. She's on the IBM Connections platform—IBM's internal social networking tools—every week, getting feedback, responding to comments, and connecting with employees. She has increased IBM's use of its pioneering "jams"—vast global brainstorms the company uses to drive deep transformation and innovation. She personally teaches a course every month on IBM's interactive Think Academy, the business world's largest massive open online course, or MOOC. She's on her iPad—perpetually—answering messages and reaching out to clients. She blogs, posts mobile videos on YouTube, and uses mobile apps to connect to and foster relationships among attendees at IBM events.[3] This combination of proactive outreach and reactive shaping allows Rometty to further her overall strategy and adjust it in real time.

Rometty and other leaders like her know the value of social and digital tools, and they use them wisely. They don't chase every bright shiny app or platform that comes along. They are successful because they take a thoughtful approach to utilizing the multitude of tools, digital and otherwise, that come and go. They use them in a focused way to listen to employees, share ideas, and engage their workforce more effectively.

Leadership has always been about the exercise of power and influence to achieve a strategic end—whether the goal is to conquer a city, launch a new product, or provide for the homeless. But what draws each of us to act on behalf of leaders is more nuanced than that. We follow people who are credible, who inspire us, and whom we trust. The relationship between leaders and followers is as fragile and complex as ever in the digital age, but something has changed of late. Technology has profoundly altered not only how we develop and nurture these relationships, but also how leadership is practiced.

In order to be truly effective today, leaders in business and society must change how they engage, and in particular how they establish and maintain relationships with their followers via digital channels. While looking someone in the eye and shaking hands with customers and employees will never lose their value, they are no longer enough to sustain relationships in a fast-moving digital world. The metamorphosis required to become what I am calling an engaged leader is not easy or painless. The openness required is unprecedented, and the trust and transparency are mind numbing for many top leaders who are accustomed to maintaining control and proceeding in an orderly and predictable fashion.

I define an engaged leader as someone who uses digital, mobile, and social tools strategically to achieve established goals as they relate to leading people and managing organizations. As basic as that sounds, putting digital skills into practice is tricky and uncomfortable. Here's what I tell leaders: If your palms aren't sweaty and your stomach isn't churning, then you probably aren't practicing engaged leadership.

Backing Off—It's Not an Option

Not everyone is comfortable stepping out from behind the safety glass of a command-and-control-style engagement in order to mingle with employees and customers in open digital venues. After all, many of today's leaders rose through the ranks by following established rules, pursuing a more traditional definition of success. The shift is disorienting and causes many leaders to shut down and disengage. It's one thing to opt out from specific channels because they are not a part of your personal plan, as Rometty has, but quite another to use inaction as your permanent default. It's as if your cell phone keeps ringing and you won't pick up.

I get it—the challenges for leaders today are daunting.

First, power and influence have decoupled from title and pay grade, and many people are at a loss as to how to proceed. The hierarchies developed at the dawn of the industrial age, and which are still common today, were done so to create efficiency and scale. They work well if you manufacture widgets, where the information and expertise needed to make decisions reside only at the top. But in our modern, digitally connected world, the need for efficiency pales compared with the need for speed, innovation, and change. The people who have to respond quickly to change live at the edges and bottom of the organization. Organizational leaders today need to trust that their employees will exercise good judgment when making decisions that in the past would have been sent "up the ladder" for someone else to make.

Next, traditional middle managers are fighting the change. Because they sit in between top leaders and the front lines, they abhor the new openness. They see top executives going around them to talk to their direct reports. They feel they are losing control, so many fight these changes tooth and nail. While these managers often present an obstacle to change, they are also a crucial part of the solution. The key for leaders is to help their lieutenants across the organization realize the fallacy of control and show them how they can be successful leaders in a networked organization.

Finally, there is a lack of ownership among leaders struggling to see the upside of the digital landscape. John F. Kennedy saw the potential in the 1960s when he was the first to use television to win over the electorate. Barack Obama, likewise, stepped up to use social networking to secure the White House and then used digital data to stay there. So why are so many CEOs and business leaders still trying to figure it out and find the upside? Because many still believe it's someone else's job. They don't think they have the skills or expertise to tap into digital and social tools. So they back off.

These are genuine challenges. But is it realistic to put on blinders and send every call to voice mail? Can leaders abdicate their responsibilities to reach out and connect, deferring to their social media team and a few intrepid Millennials? No way—not if they want to have a functioning, robust relationship with customers, colleagues, and employees. There is a many-to-one high-speed connection today between leaders and followers, and this new structure requires new tools. The pace of technological innovation, explained famously by Moore's law, has produced a number of drivers (see Figure I.1). They explain this complex state of affairs and begin to spell out the opportunities for the bold and the brave. You've seen these drivers before; let's look at what they mean to leaders.

Figure I.1: Drivers of Digital Transformation

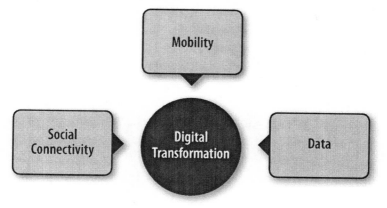

The most obvious driver is connectivity. The rise of social networks means that we can be immediately linked. We can find each other and make contact with anyone—poor or powerful—fairly easily. Anonymity is impossible, and exclusivity diminished. Networks enable us to work together fluidly across space and time. The result is a rise of agency for individuals. Conversely, the power of hierarchies has markedly declined. All this together means that leaders have no place to hide. They need to be prepared to respond to and interact with the masses in a way that would have made King George VI faint dead away. The corresponding promise, of course, is mythic: Leaders now have a direct link to customers.

Mobility is another fundamental driver that's changed the game for leaders. Thanks to an array of technology, your team can work just about anywhere in the world without sacrificing speed and performance. This offers leaders instant access to a much wider pool of talent. It also diminishes their ability to control and micromanage. Despite the strong urge to push back and say, "No way!" to remote access and unlimited mobility, it's impossible to stem the swirling tide of change. Leaders need to jump in and use digital tools to stay connected to an increasingly mobile and global workforce. How else can they cut through the noise, communicate expectations, and develop relationships with people across time zones?

The final driver worth mentioning is big data. In the past, a knowledge gap separated the people who posed the strategic questions—leaders—and the data analysts who parsed bits and bytes. Today, accessing data is much easier, and the analysis is automated. This enables executives to ask many more questions and find the answers themselves. What's more, big data allows them to work *faster*. The best example I can think of is IBM's Watson Analytics. Because Watson Analytics learns while evaluating unstructured data so rapidly, it is capable of returning natural-language search queries instantly with evidence-based hypotheses. For example, I can ask it, "Which of my salespeople are most effective at using industry content to engage our customers?" As amazing as it sounds, Watson Analytics has the answer. Although not all leaders have access to Watson-quality data parsing just yet, it's coming.

These three drivers have at least two important things in common. First, they are forcing top leaders to rethink their place in the organization and grab hold of digital tools to help them make decisions and get things done. Second, despite the challenges just described, they offer huge opportunities and momentous upside for leaders willing to take the leap.

About This Book—Listen, Share, and Engage

I've spent considerable time working with executives—in small groups and large public venues—researching solutions and designing tools to help them develop digital skills and strategies. I've written two previous books on the topic and have field-tested numerous ideas, dashboards, and practical models. For the purposes of this book, I have distilled much of my advice on engaged leadership into the three steps that leaders should take to successfully hasten their digital transformation: listen, share, and engage (see Figure I.2).

These three steps work together to create a runway for engaged leaders to accomplish their goals. Listening is the way leaders determine what individuals need from them to enhance the relationship and deepen the connection. Sharing is how leaders use stories and other tools to develop mutual understanding and shape people's mind-sets and thus the actions they take. And engagement is a two-way dialogue that motivates and mobilizes

Figure I.2. Framework for Digital Leadership Transformation

followers to act in concert toward a common purpose. As we will see, the nature of the online medium means that the idea of a follower is broader than ever. One's followers are not only employees but also customers, peers, and the people in one's wider networks. In other words, effectively leveraging digital channels increases a leader's power and influence exponentially.

We will explore each of the three steps in detail in the chapters that follow.

1. Listen at Scale

We know that listening is a fundamental part of developing relationships. It helps us understand what people are interested in and where they are coming from. In a sense, the best talkers are also the best listeners. We see this everywhere we go. We can't walk in and engage a group at a networking event or a conference luncheon unless we initially stop to listen—who is in the conversation, what are their concerns, what are they talking about? With that information you can enter the fray and steer the conversation in a strategic way. The same is true for many types of dialogue—listen first and then share.

The ancient art of listening takes on new meaning in the digital age. We can listen to tens, hundreds, or thousands of people all at once without ever looking them in the eye. And we can do this on a continual basis—at scale. With technology we can listen to our direct reports down the hall, front-line employees down the street, and project teams across the globe. We can listen for ideas, opinions, and complaints. We can also listen to what employees are saying about the organization—to us directly and to each other on public social networks. It's an awesome new world when we can tune in so easily and deeply—but it is also a noisy and distracting world without the proper filters.

As we will see in Chapter 1, there is an art and science to listening in the digital age. The art of listening entails choosing who and what to listen to in order to accomplish the goals you've set forth, whereas the science of listening involves utilizing certain tools and techniques that are proven, effective ways to focus a leader's attention on what matters and to avoid information overload.

2. Share to Shape

Like listening, sharing is a fundamental skill—and a basic developmental milestone that starts in childhood. Over time we learn to share as a way to build trust and cultivate relationships in all aspects of our lives. We say that people who don't share close themselves off from others and become socially isolated, while those who proceed in the other extreme, oversharing, watch their efforts at openness backfire as people back away from them. Sharing needs to be balanced and strategic.

Much of that strategic balance is lost in traditional hier-archies, where sharing is rigidly structured and constrained. Each layer of an organization is designed to filter information up and push decisions down. And that doesn't make a lot of sense. After all, if you examine all the information within a company, maybe 1% or 2% of it truly needs to be kept under lock and key:

mergers and acquisitions, compensation, and the secret sauce (e.g. the formula for Coke). Yet we teach leaders that in order to be successful, they must hoard information to enhance their own value.

The opposite is true in a networked organization where sharing is a net positive. When leaders share, they engage and attract followers. In Chapter 2 we will examine how leaders can use new ways of sharing to inspire people to follow their lead. In essence, leaders become facilitators who accelerate the spread of information and shape the decision-making process. As part of that, we will look at the art of sharing—including what content to share and how to shape it with strategic intent. In addition, we will explore how to make something more shareable utilizing emotion, authenticity, and uniqueness. (The ALS Ice Bucket Challenge is a perfect example of something that became shareable. So many people—leaders included—accepted the challenge because it was authentic, important, portable, and engaging.) We will explore the science of sharing as well, by looking at the digital tools that are at a leader's disposal.

The upshot of this type of sharing is that people will stop grasping at what you, the leader, are looking for. They can stop guessing what you are thinking. Instead they will *know* what you want and expect, and they can focus on delivering it.

3. Engage to Transform

Data from Gallup shows that only 13% of people worldwide are engaged at work, meaning emotionally invested in creating value for their organizations.[4] And despite many companies' best efforts to address this problem, that number has barely budged since 2010.[5] In other research, we've seen that engagement occurs when people feel appreciated for a job well done. Long-term satisfaction is less about raw compensation and more about being on the team and part of something important. Yet, historically, engagement within organizations has been inefficient and haphazard. Leaders could reach out and personally shake hands with only a few people at a time, or perhaps a few hundred through town hall meetings. Now, in the networked world, the constraints of time and space are largely eliminated. Leaders can personally engage with individuals or groups through multiple touch points, thereby cultivating and transforming relationships purposefully. Discussions can be far more fluid, leading to a deeper ongoing relationship that aligns people around common objectives. Engagement, after all, is a strategic type of dialogue that extends beyond engaging employees to engaging customers, partners, and shareholders of every stripe.

For the engaged leader, the *art* of engagement includes deciding when and how to connect with followers in a focused way. As we will see, engagement in the digital age needs to be orchestrated. The *science*, again, is about using digital tools to achieve a specific goal and putting in enough practice to become proficient. Wash, rinse, repeat.

The three parts of our model—Listen at Scale, Share to Shape, and Engage to Transform—are fluid, and overlap: We listen in advance of sharing, and share as a way to engage. Separately, as well as in concert, these steps are designed to help leaders develop their instincts, skills, and confidence. They will also guide institutions—businesses, communities, and schools—on how to develop and nurture digitally engaged leaders.

With that in mind, Chapters 1, 2, 3 each examines and unpacks one of the three steps of the engaged leadership framework. They further introduce the main ideas and present a plan for execution. Chapter 4 puts the pieces together and builds an even bigger model for implementation across organizations.

Becoming an Engaged Leader—
Strategy Begins with a Plan

Leadership, compared to finance and perhaps marketing, is associated with the softer side of business. But with technology we can sprinkle some rigor into the mix. A primary takeaway running through this book is that leadership in the digital age can be more effective and more strategic. More effective because leaders can cultivate relationships with followers in ways that were simply not possible in the past; more strategic because the new tools are tailor-made to help leaders reach their objectives. This benefits leaders by guiding them to focus their efforts appropriately, and it advances organizations because it is scalable.

Becoming an engaged leader requires a transformation in how you think, how you work, and the types of relationships you are comfortable cultivating. But before that can begin, leaders must have the right tools for the task. There are two questions packed in here. First, *what is the right goal or objective?* Having a hammer won't help a carpenter unless she knows where to place the nail. What are your objectives? What problem or challenge will you ask digital tools to solve? Second, *what are the right tools for the task?* Having the nail in the right spot won't help our carpenter if she has a wrench instead of a hammer. Many leaders use apps and social networks (Yammer, Twitter, etc.) because they think they should—they've read about them or a savvy colleague uses them. Alternately, many leaders frequent one social site over another simply because they feel comfortable there.

When it comes to digital leadership, one size does not fit all. In order to assign the right tools for the right task, and vice versa, we will use a worksheet as the basis for creating your digital transformation plan. A downloadable version of the worksheet is available at charleneli.com/the-engaged-leader. At the end of each chapter, you'll have a chance to fill out this worksheet in more depth and detail. To get started, identify up to three strategic goals you want to accomplish, and the measurement you will use to track your goal attainment. Included in Figure I.3 are three example business goals that we will use at the end of Chapters 1 through 3 to illustrate in a tangible way how listening, sharing, and engaging support business goals.

It's important to note that your digital transformation is a personal journey. The ideas and tools in this book will catalyze the transformation, but the shift in mind-set is just as important. There are no perfect off-the-shelf methods for how to proceed. People always ask me, "What's tomorrow's Snapchat or Twitter?" I don't know what it is—but it will be there. In some ways it does not matter what it is—it's simply another round of disruption. People want to chase and touch the latest bright shiny object. They think they need to stay on top of it. I tell leaders, "Above all, don't get distracted." Engaged leadership means not chasing the

Figure I.3.
Example Worksheet: Identify Goals and Measurement

Goal	Attract and retain the best people in the industry.	Grow market share in our new target market.	Create an extraordinary experience for our customers.
Measurement	Improve retention rate to 90%.	Grow share to 25% of addressable market.	Increase customer satisfaction by 25%.
Listen at Scale			
Share to Shape			
Engage to Transform			

latest apps and gadgets. Being an engaged leader in the digital era means knowing what your goals are and what tools to use to achieve them. It also means being brave and bold enough to step into the fray: listen to followers, share yourself with them, and engage them directly in new and amazing ways.

CHAPTER 1

Listen at Scale

The Denver-based chain Red Robin launched its Pig Out Burger at casual dining outlets across the United States in 2012. The sandwich was fully loaded with cheese, onions, bacon, aioli, and two fire-grilled beef patties. This meat lover's menu item should have had carnivores swooning across all 50 states. Only, it didn't, and the complaints began streaming in. *The bacon is soggy and greasy. The aioli is drippy and weak. The bun is falling apart in customers' hands.* As the reviews flooded in, they were funneled to the test kitchens at headquarters. "Managers started talking about ways to tweak the Pig Out recipe, and four weeks later, we had an improved, kitchen-tested version to roll out to restaurants," Chris Laping, CIO and senior vice president of business transformation reports. "That's a process that would have taken 12 to 18 months before."[6]

Executives acted fast and with precision, and that's notable. But there's more to the story. It wasn't *customers* who were writing the reviews about the burger. It was Red Robin employees. Restaurant servers posted what they heard from customers and experienced themselves via the company's internal social network. They shared their concerns and experiences online, and executives were all ears. They took an interest, asked for more details, and worked with employees to solve the problem. Leaders listened and responded. Red Robin CEO Steve Carley comments, "If you engage staff in a way that shows their opinion is important, it's extraordinary what you learn—and the excitement you generate."[7]

As the Red Robin example illustrates, and what most of us know intuitively, listening is instrumental in cultivating relationships. In this case, leaders listened, employees felt heard, and it made a positive difference in the business. In any setting, organizational or otherwise, listening delivers *context* and *knowledge* about the speaker. The deeper you listen, the stronger the connection becomes, and the easier it is to develop and manage the relationship.

Without context and knowledge, it is impossible to be on the same page as the people you lead. We've all seen this dynamic at play at cocktail parties. In most cases you can't walk in and commandeer the conversations. First, you need to stop to pay attention. Who's talking? What are their interests and concerns? What are they buzzing about? Then you can enter the conversation, forge a connection, and strategically shape the conversation. The same holds true in relationships between leaders and followers. Listening allows leaders to better understand the people they want to lead, externally as well as internally. It enables them to know those people's likes and dislikes, leverage their knowledge, and improve results in the way that we saw at Red Robin.

All this is just as true today as ever. But what's interesting about the digital space is that now you can listen at *scale* (see Figure 1.1). Your customers, employees, partners, and shareholders are constantly talking on digital and social platforms: They are talking to you. They are talking to each other *about* you. They are sharing ideas, impressions, and concerns about your business. They are complimenting, complaining, and engaging at all hours in a dazzling array of voices and styles. And yes, you can listen, respond, and react not only to one person at a time but to hundreds or thousands or more. The key is that you listen *with your eyes* to many people all at once, anytime, and from anyplace. That is listening at scale.

Figure 1.1. Listen at Scale

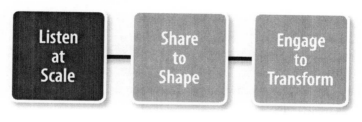

In the past we could only scratch the surface of listening. A person might tell you one thing and say something else to their peers. But now you can know with much greater certainty what people think and what's really going on in the space around you. While listening is considered polite, thoughtful, and empathetic, it's also a power play. Leaders who listen are in a position to exert their influence and shape positive business outcomes.

A New Mind-Set for Listening

Listening at scale creates new opportunities for leaders. Yet, in order to fully activate these opportunities, we need to undergo a shift in how we think about the ways we listen. The first opportunity that comes with listening at scale is *access*. In the past, CEOs and senior executives relied on direct reports to feed them information and intelligence. This ivory tower approach was counterproductive for a number of reasons. It kept leaders at a distance and insulated them from the front line of business. It also forced them to trust direct reports to bring in adequate intelligence from the field. Yet, as we recall from the child's game of telephone, secondhand information is delivered with a subjective spin, and the original context often gets lost in translation.

This arm's-length dynamic causes leaders to become disconnected from reality, and leaves them scratching their heads and wondering, *Is that really what's going on out there?* One of the great advantages of crossing over to become an engaged leader is that executives can see (for themselves) what is happening all around them. This new normal is not only refreshing for leaders, but also empowering. They can survey the chatter and interpret it on their own, thereby eliminating the middleman and avoiding the associated spin.

A second opportunity that has come with listening at scale is *relationship building*. Digital listening brings with it an unprecedented level of certainty when it comes to getting to know one's followers. In the past you had to guess what was important to people and surmise what they were thinking. Now you can know—because there are so many more ways to listen. In addition, it's not one-to-one relationship building. Engaged leaders can listen at scale and hear what the entire organization, as well as the wider ecosystem, is telling them.

The third opportunity that listening at scale has brought to leadership is characterized by *constancy*. In the past, listening came in big chunks—quarterly reports and annual surveys forced executives to listen. They would go out and talk to customers and employees as part of a road show that lasted for a few weeks out of the year. The biggest mind-set change associated with listening at scale is that listening now has to happen 24/7. Leaders are expected to tune in on a regular basis. They can't look away for a few days or a week or they'll miss something important. And they can't defer this task to anyone else.

There is an art and a science to listening at scale, and we will examine both.

The Art of Listening

The art of listening at scale has everything to do with making strategic choices. Focusing your efforts requires a mix of judgment and intuition. It also requires a strategic mind-set. Once again, it begins by knowing your goals. Later in the chapter we will examine specific tools for listening, but there isn't one precise algorithm that reveals exactly where and when to direct your everyday listening efforts. Listening "with your eyes" across multiple channels entails endless opportunities and combinations. You can tap into project notes, sales intelligence, employee chatter, and industry analysis. You can listen to key customer groups or employees on the front line, or narrow your gaze to listen to direct reports or new business leads. It's up to you.

Listening at scale is not about listening to everybody. Beyond strategy and intuition, there are a number of techniques to help hone the art of listening at scale and narrow down your efforts.

Use People as Your Filters

Without filters, listening at scale can be overwhelming—particularly for leaders accustomed to having information fed to them in neat little packages at regular intervals. The most organic way to separate the signals from the noise is to rely on the people around you who are able to hone in on what matters and let the rest go. We all have individuals in our network whom we turn to when we want to find out what's really going on. Some people know about finance and fiduciary responsibility, say, while others are hooked into art and architecture. These and others like them are the people you should be listening to.

Leaders, therefore, don't need to read everything—they need to follow and listen to other people who read everything. And our best conduits of information aren't necessarily other leaders and executives. Frequently we need to look farther afield. It may be that someone on the IT help desk connects with people across different departments. Perhaps there is one particular sales manager who's expert at pulling together the loose ends to offer a complete picture of the business. Or maybe a key customer has a blog that provides the best industry insights. These people serve as excellent filters. Follow them on Twitter or on your internal social network. Add them to your network on LinkedIn. Whatever, just listen to what they are saying, posting, and broadcasting.

Listen through the Layers

Just as there are different people to listen to, there are also numerous frequencies that are wide open for listening—different layers, if you will:

- **Active versus passive listening.** Active listening is listening head-on through your own systems and networks—the company Facebook page, the tweets @YourCompany, as well as your internal social networking tools. Passive listening is monitoring less specific outside targets—industry news and RSS feeds—and seeing what patterns emerge. Both these layers provide differing (or sometimes corresponding) perspectives that equal one part of the whole story.

- **Direct versus indirect listening.** Direct listening means tuning into what people tell you directly—that is, anything that is targeted at you. Indirect listening is capturing what people are saying to other people or to each other. With indirect listening, you're listening to things that they may not consciously be choosing to share with you—but it's out there, so why not listen?

- **Inside versus outside the stream.** Listen inside the stream by reading Twitter or LinkedIn news feeds. Listen outside the stream by reading comments, retweets, and the like (content that is posted about content).

Keeping all these layers of listening in mind helps leaders piece together a complete picture of their business and decide where they want to focus their everyday efforts.

Scan Your Environment

Before we look at specific tools to help leaders act on what they hear, a final technique for practicing the art of listening at scale is simply to scan your environment regularly for a few minutes several times a day. Make it a habit.

This is something David Thodey, the CEO of Australia's telecom giant Telstra, does.[8] Each morning, Thodey, a renowned early riser, grabs a cup of coffee and his device. He looks through his enterprise social network on Yammer to review the overnight activity. He scans it to see what the general vibe of the organization is. Scrolling down Telstra's activity feed allows him to quickly see which ideas or dilemmas are generating a lot of discussion, which are important. He follows certain people—connectors and idea generators throughout the organization. Looking at their posts allows him to see which topics have traction and where the real problems lie. More often than not, he'll post in those discussions to keep them moving and give them visibility with senior leaders. He has described Yammer as "the greatest hierarchy buster I've ever seen."[9]

Thodey checks in again at lunchtime, and at the end of the day, to see if there is anything emerging that needs his attention. Sometimes he uses what he reads to finalize the agenda of his regular staff meetings. He'll go in and say, "So, I just saw on Yammer that there's an interesting discussion going on over here. Is it something we need to look into?" Oftentimes, because his senior leadership team knows that he's looking and listening, they are already on top of it. So much so that the platform is referred to in some quarters as "Ask David" rather than Yammer.

According to Thodey, he doesn't worry about having to see and read everything—listening doesn't carry the burden of obligation that a full email in-box does. Rather, it's a way of getting a taste, savored in small bits throughout the day, one that gives him the knowledge to make better decisions.

The Science of Listening at Scale

Many leaders opt out of practicing the art of listening because they think it's too time-consuming. There's too much data, and it's overwhelming. Yet the reality is that being digital is fast becoming mandatory. Expectations have changed, and followers assume that you will be up to date on what they share on social sites. *You don't know that people are talking about the plant closures? It's all over our feed. (Aren't you paying attention?)* If you care about establishing, maintaining, and deepening your relationships with employees, colleagues, and team members, you need to be listening to them and making adjustments based on what you hear.

Luckily there are excellent and accessible tools that leaders can use to organize themselves, prevent data overload, and separate the signal from the noise. This is the science side of listening at scale. Until recently this was considered to be a job for IT leaders and chief marketing officers (CMOs). But the tools and apps today are so powerful and easy to use that leaders themselves can apply them and have a front-row seat to what is going on across their business and industry.

The tools you choose to use for listening must connect directly to your strategic leadership goals. Once you identify the top three things you need to manage and monitor with social and digital tools, it's time to get started. But remember, not every leader needs to light up the Twittersphere or have a working mastery of Snapchat. There are RSS feeds, social networks, microblogs, vlogs, ambient alerts, content aggregators, dashboards, and filters. It all depends upon what you need to achieve. If you do use Twitter, great ... but use it strategically. Listening at scale does not mean following everyone who follows you. (That's the least productive thing any leader can do.) The question, then, becomes how to listen based on your goals and the needs of the people you want to lead.

Regardless of the specifics of any individual situation, there are a number techniques and tools that all leaders should consider as a way to get organized for the science of listening at scale.

Create Content Filters

We've talked about creating filters to make listening at scale more manageable. As mentioned, the people you trust most may be your best filters. Find a small group of influencers in your organization or network whom you respect. Maybe these people are the connectors who cut across silos and intersect with a wide cross section of your organization. Follow them and find out whom they follow, what social networks they populate, and what streams they are listening to. Most internal enterprise social networks (such as Chatter, Connections, Socialcast, tibbr, and Yammer) allow users to see whom other people are following. External sites like Twitter are the same—you can see whom other people are listening to. If your team members are all listening to some of the same people, you will want to check them out.

Directing your listening is a trial-and-error endeavor. It will take a few weeks of tweaks before you feel satisfied that you are listening to the right people and finding the feeds that give you what you need to lead. RSS feeds are useful for pushing blogs, feeds, and industry news in your direction, but they need to be filtered (narrowed down to suit your interests) and aggregated (organized so that you can scan through them easily).

Platforms such as Twitter allow you to filter and personalize content by name or key word. Yet this can get tedious if you need to do it on a number of different platforms. There are better ways. Content filters such as Feed Rinse, for example, allow you to screen multiple feeds, block posts by key word, or tag content. For example, if you want to hear the chatter about big data but want steer away from posts and comments about a particular news item, these types of filters will customize your feeds.

Filters help leaders focus their efforts and get the greatest return given their limited time and attention. Likewise, there are additional tools that leaders can use to optimize information. For instance, I use an app on my phone called Refresh that helps me prepare for meetings. When I have an appointment with someone, it populates my calendar entries with background knowledge about that person, synced from the Web, including past jobs and career highlights from LinkedIn and elsewhere. If I am meeting with Susan about a project, I can see if she has tweeted about that project. If I am meeting with an internal job candidate, I will be able to see his past job experience right on my calendar.

These are the types of tools that save leaders time and direct them to what they really need to monitor each day. In addition, they enable the type of focused listening that would otherwise take endless hours to achieve.

Listen across Multiple Channels: Dashboards and Command Centers

After identifying whom and what they'll listen to, the next step for leaders is to funnel the information into a format they can readily use. That's where content aggregators come in. Content aggregators (such as Feedly) combine feeds and streams to create a dashboard—one page to scroll through, thereby saving you from going from link to link across the Web. Feedly is effective because it monitors activity across your networks and highlights posts and news items that are most popular among your colleagues so you don't miss anything that's trending. Another useful dashboard for leaders is Hootsuite. Instead of going from LinkedIn, to Twitter, to Facebook, Hootsuite brings all these to one place and organizes them across channels. Content streams can then be organized by followers, company names, hashtags, or key words. You can also create interactive dashboards that generate data-rich reports.

Some leaders create their own dashboards to suit their particular needs. The shipping company Maersk Line, for example, maps content and information by relationship—comments and posts by employees, industry experts, customers, and fans of the company are all tracked separately and compared (see Figure 1.2). Maersk even created a platform for its "fans" to congregate so the company can listen to what they say. And it engages an additional 800 shipping industry experts using a LinkedIn Group called "Shipping Circle." Simple and ingenious. Maersk figured out where each of its constituents liked to congregate, channel by channel, and built a science around listening carefully to the conversations.[10]

Any dashboard you create on your own is going to look different from someone else's—design depends entirely on the goals you have in mind. Regardless, Maersk Line's is a great example of specialized listening. Maersk doesn't listen to all the chatter everywhere; it tracks particular groups of people where they hang out. In the end, Maersk Line is listening to followers and using the information it collects to run its business.

Figure 1.2. Maersk Line's Audience Mapping

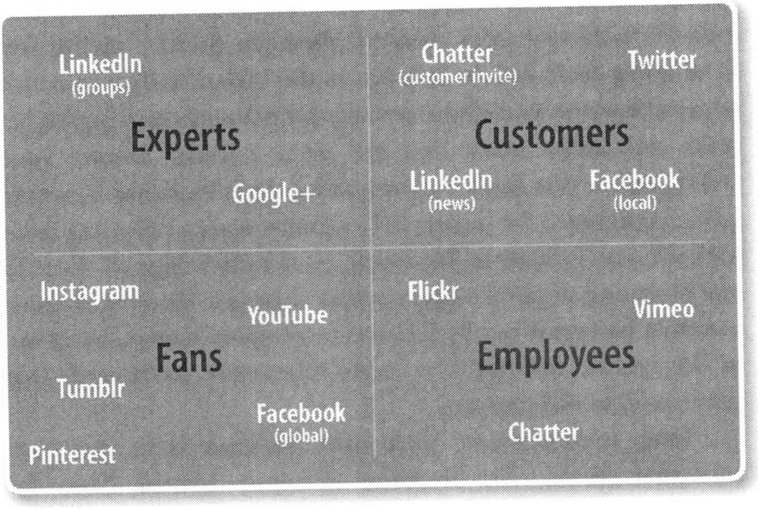

Spend 15 Minutes Listening

The final step in the science of listening is adding a guardrail around *when* you listen. Leaders need parameters, or one of two things can happen: They don't prioritize listening, or they go off the rails and listen too much for too long.

I tell leaders to get into the habit of listening every day so they have a continual drip of the information they need almost in real time. They don't need to dedicate a lot of time. People are accustomed to approaching listening online with an in-box mentality. If someone sends you a text, you answer it. You have to read every text or you'll miss something important. But it's different with listening at scale. You don't need to read everything—merely skim through to get a feel for things. The effort should be light and quick, just to get a sense of what people are talking about.

When leaders ask me how much time they should spend listening each day, I suggest *no more than 15 minutes.* And the time doesn't need to be scheduled. Instead, get in the habit of dedicating your interstitial time to reading the feed and perusing your dashboard. I'm talking about the in-between time—moments in the cab, standing in line at Starbucks, or waiting for your lunch order. This is just listening—this is not sharing. It's not writing a blog or tweeting—it's just checking your feeds.

You know how powerful those 15 minutes can make you? They can make you incredibly smart and informed. If you use the time wisely, it may turn out to be the best 15 minutes of your day in terms of return on investment.

Listening for Power and Influence

Listening delivers knowledge. Maersk Line knows not only what its employees are thinking, but also what its customers, fans, and industry experts are saying. It uses that knowledge to create compensation packages for new recruits and to design its next generation of ships. The more information you have about your employees and followers, the better position you'll be in to build those relationships and exert influence.

The same is true for the other two parts of the engaged leader model. We'll see that sharing can be used to shape outcomes, and engagement can mobilize followers to act on your behalf.

Take a few minutes to think through how you can listen at scale to accomplish your strategic goals. Describe whom or what you need to listen to in order to accomplish each of your goals. Identify any tools, resources, or training you may need to do this. Figure 1.3 identifies some ways that listening can support the example goals identified in the introduction.

Figure 1.3. Example Worksheet: Listen at Scale

Goal	Attract and retain the best people in the industry.	Grow market share in our new target market.	Create an extraordinary experience for our customers.
Measurement	Improve retention rate to 90%.	Grow share to 25% of addressable market.	Increase customer satisfaction by 25%.
Listen at Scale	**Look for ideas trending on internal digital platform.**	**Monitor the Twittersphere for ideas to serve the target market.**	**Listen (with your eyes) for trending— complaints and kudos on the company Facebook page.**
Share to Shape			
Engage to Transform			

Questions to Get Started

- What information do you need in order to be successful?
- What is most important to hear and learn from customers, employees, partners, suppliers, and shareholders?
- Who are the people you need and want to listen to? How will digital tools help you listen to them?
- What decisions do you want to make based on the information?
- What are some ways that you would choose to listen at scale?

CHAPTER 2

Share to Shape

Sharing to shape is seldom a one-size-fits-all endeavor. On the one hand, consider a certain leader I've encountered— Rosemary. She uses Twitter to connect with her sprawling team, categorizing them into groups such as managers and supervisors, and she uses its direct-messaging capabilities to connect with them. Unorthodox, perhaps, but it works for her because Twitter is easy to access from anywhere and universally popular among her staff as well as the heads of HR, engineering, and business development. She uses it to recognize employee accomplishments, set and reinforce expectations, and share business intelligence, crucial safety tips, and even timely updates on traffic and weather.

Francis, on the other hand, is half a world away from Rosemary and prefers photos to text. He broadcasts the occasional blog or Facebook update through his marketing team, but his chosen medium for sharing is "selfies." He's perpetually on the road at speaking engagements, and selfies, therefore, are how he connects on the fly with the people he meets all around the world.

What do Rosemary and Francis have in common? Quite a bit despite their differing responsibilities and social media preferences. Rosemary is Rosemary Turner, president of UPS North California District, who is charged with overseeing 17,000 employees—every manager, staff member, driver, and dispatcher in the territory.[11] If the trucks don't roll or if Christmas gifts

Figure 2.1. Share to Shape

don't get delivered, it's on Rosemary. Francis is Pope Francis, the reigning head of the Catholic Church. He is Bishop of Rome and Vatican City as well as the leader of approximately 1.1 billion parishioners worldwide. He meets with heads of state and maintains diplomatic relationships with more than 100 nations, all while trying to forge a consistent dialogue with Catholics around the world.

Beyond a shared concern for maintaining Christmas traditions, both are engaged leaders who understand how to harness social tools for sharing in a way that helps them manage relationships and shape the actions of their many followers. As we examined in Chapter 1, listening at scale enables leaders to determine what ideas, information, or actions will inspire followership. Sharing, then, is how engaged leaders not only attract followers but also keep them effective and productive vis-à-vis the leaders' wider objectives (see Figure 2.1).

Why Sharing Shapes

Leaders who are less sure about sharing than Turner and the pontiff commonly ask me, *How do I generate followers?* And I typically respond, *Well, you're already leading people, right?* The perceived disconnect between everyday leadership and followership within social channels belies an interesting and relevant point. Leaders may have 500 or 5,000 people reporting to them, but only a tiny percentage of those people follow them on social and digital channels. This highlights a number of significant opportunities that sharing, as presented here, holds for leaders. Sharing, the next step to becoming an engaged leader, can exponentially multiply one's authority and influence in several ways.

First, sharing *forges connections with followers* that improve relationships. At UPS, for example, Turner's biggest concern each day is supporting employees on the move across San Francisco's main arteries. Twitter links her easily and instantly to thousands of drivers out in the field in trucks or to sales executives visiting major accounts. It's a platform that UPS employees are comfortable with because many were already using it to connect with each other. *Stay away from the Bay Bridge—there's an accident*; *Remember, the Giants game starts at 5:30*; and so

---

Figure 2.2. Rosemary Turner Tweet Recognizing an Employee

on. Figure 2.2 shows an example of Turner recognizing a UPS employee on Twitter for work well done.

The insight and intelligence that Turner shares across her domain allows her to connect informally with people across the organization. She uses Twitter to broadcast to everyone at all levels of the company. Because of the goodwill she has established through sharing, and the way that she shares, employees feel validated, and Turner's influence within UPS is elevated. Because of what she shares in social channels, her people trust her, and the credibility she has earned pays dividends that allow her to build followership and shape performance.

Second, sharing helps leaders *achieve key objectives.* As with listening, sharing must be geared to accomplish strategic goals or else it risks becoming superfluous. One of Turner's goals is to empower employees across her unit to speak up with their ideas and concerns. She wants to level the playing field to improve operations. This dovetails with the wider "open-door policy" at UPS, whereby employees, customers, and vendors are encouraged to maintain an open dialogue with company leadership. She shared, "I am finding that when I send out a blast on Twitter, I get just as much if not more reaction than if I send out a survey internally. One manager who is four levels below me said, 'Rosemary, I respectfully disagree.' I really like that kind of unfiltered honesty and I'm trying to get more of that kind of engagement from our people."[12] Turner's approach to sharing enables employees to reach her anytime—thereby achieving her goals as well as the larger corporate mandate for openness.

Interestingly, Turner was not always so enthusiastic about sharing. Two years ago, when her communications leader suggested that she try out social media, Turner's first thought was "I'm not Kim Kardashian—I'm not going to post what I had for lunch!"[13] In the end, she acquiesced, but insisted that her communications person run the Twitter account on Turner's behalf. When those initial posts started getting great reviews, Turner realized that Twitter was a game changer. She shared, "The impact has been dramatic. I feel I can touch people and it extends the impact of my leadership when I listen, and then share back what I'm hearing. I now have all of these connections, where I can contact someone and find out what I want."[14]

Similarly, one of Pope Francis's goals is to connect with common people in order to make the teachings of Catholicism more accessible. Every time he steps away from the bulletproof Popemobile or comes down from the balcony to stride solo across St. Peter's Square, he is working toward that mandate. Everything he does is carefully crafted to support this goal, and he uses social media strategically to extend his reach. He chooses selfies as his mode of sharing because they correspond with his objectives.

Finally, sharing also *amplifies a leader's power and influence.* As what she shares gets passed around, her sphere of influence can extend well beyond the official confines of her department or domain.

These are just a few of the positive by-products of transforming into an engaged leader.

The Sharing Shift—From Scarcity to Abundance

Each stage in becoming an engaged leader—listening, sharing, and engaging—gets progressively more complicated in terms of navigating change and risk. While Millennials and digital natives are accustomed to sharing all aspects of themselves with their virtual friends, today's top leaders seldom share the same passion for openness. And that makes sense when you consider the dramatic shift in the supply-and-demand dynamics of information.

Leaders in the past accumulated power by hoarding information and then releasing it in a highly controlled way, thereby creating scarcity. Today they can be far more influential by disseminating information more broadly (harnessing abundance). Although leaders shouldn't be capricious in how they share, today's inherent loss of control creates a condition of permanent uncertainty that they need to acclimate to (and perhaps even learn to appreciate). The process starts by breaking down the waves of change associated with sharing in order to examine them in manageable chunks:

1. **From talking at people to sharing with them.** This shift is closely aligned with the power dynamic just described. Leaders of old, in commander-in-chief mode, would direct others to act, offering sparse context around end goals and little latitude with regard to execution. Today, with the proliferation of knowledge, sharing needs to start from a desire to help followers achieve their goals in addition to your own. The key is to clearly articulate the overall strategy so that everyone can coalesce around a common purpose. Sharing needs to *inspire* action as opposed to dictating the precise shape that action takes.

2. **From infrequent reporting to continuous sharing.** Leaders recall the premium they placed, circa 1990, on quarterly shareholder reports and the mythic unveiling of year-end results. Weeks of resources were dedicated to crafting one perfect presentation that happened on schedule and according to the calendar. Well, that was before analytics and real-time information opened the floodgates. Today, leaders need to share, and frequently, just to stay in front of the message.

Rosemary Turner is sharing all day every day on multiple platforms. Why? In large part because it keeps her mammoth workforce on track. The flip side is that without her advice, employees would look in ten different directions for guidance and end up at odds with one another. Keeping the trucks running on time is especially important in a logistics business such as UPS. Regardless, frequent sharing keeps people aligned and in sync.

3. **From formal to informal sharing.** In part because of the frequency just described, informal sharing has become the norm. No longer can leaders emerge from the ivory tower, put out some finely crafted pearls of wisdom, and expect followers and direct reports to hang on their every word. The world moves too fast for that sort of formality. Even the papacy has taken notice. Francis seldom offers proclamations from the balcony or even from behind the pulpit. Instead he walks among the people or drives around in his (very) used car—190,000+ miles—all the while stopping to pose for photographs.

4. **From polished to imperfect.** This mode of sharing is perhaps the most difficult change for some leaders to make. Sharing, because it is ongoing and informal, is also oftentimes off-the-cuff. When opportunities to share were infrequent, whatever you shared needed to be finely honed. Now, with the time required to broadcast drastically streamlined, the friction is removed from sharing, and informality is the norm. Luckily your posts need not be perfect; instead they should be authentic, relevant, and timely—photos, reactions, and a few choice words that suit the moment.

These shifts in sharing norms leave leaders feeling vulnerable. *What if people don't like how I share? What if I share the wrong thing?* Even worse: *What if nobody cares?*

As we will see as we go deeper into the art and science of sharing to shape, any one tweet is neither a home run nor a black mark. The cumulative effect is what matters. Sharing is the foundation for building relationships, accumulating and connecting with followers, and shaping behavior in a strategic way.

The Art of Sharing

Fast, frequent, and informal makes it all sound simple, but admittedly there is an art to sharing that requires cultivation. In taking a deeper dive into relevant tips and techniques, we will examine the types of things that leaders can and should share as well as how to present these for the greatest impact.

At a fundamental level, successful sharing connects to three things: strategic goals, common ground, and relationship focus. Leaders should share with a purpose in mind. Engaged leadership is a strategic endeavor. What and how you share always corresponds with the goals you've set forth for yourself as a leader and for your organization. In addition, the common ground and shared interests you glean through listening at scale play a key part in informing the types of things you share. Sometimes sharing may be as simple as responding to emerging concerns before they become serious issues; other times it will be a direct appeal to followers for ideas or input. Regardless, both of these require listening before sharing.

As for the relationship focus, at each phase in becoming an engaged leader, we return to the basic question—what type of relationship do I want to have with followers? That is where the art comes into play.

Take the case of Padmasree Warrior, chief technology and strategy officer for Cisco. Warrior has raised sharing to an art form more than almost anyone else I've seen. She shares constantly with 1.5 million Twitter followers from across her widely diverse network.[15] Part of her goal is to be a cheerleader for Cisco, and she's swift at disseminating research and products related to "the internet of things," among other Cisco priority projects. But does Cisco's intellectual property really have what it takes to appeal to so many people around the Twittersphere? Probably not. Warrior also posts frequently on topics that are important to her personally—immigration reform, philanthropy, women in technology, and even art.[16] She posts photos of her own paintings and shares poetry, particularly haikus.[17] Her approach to social media is authentic and thick with her personal perspective on life—and this candor deepens the relationships she has with her followers. They appreciate her unique spin on topics. The result: Warrior gets Cisco messaging in front of thousands of people who ordinarily would find little interest of in tech talk.

The sharing style of Warrior (along with that of others whose style we will examine) offers a cross section of best practices in the art of sharing.

Sharing That Spreads—Emotion, Authenticity, Point of View

There are three things you should strive for in your sharing: emotion, authenticity, and point of view. Warrior's tweets are often repeated and retweeted outside her own web of followers and certainly beyond Cisco's spheres of interest. Her messages spread out and take hold because they have authenticity. She speaks from the heart, and her point of view is evident in every post. In one post, she artfully melded insights into self-expression and transparency (see Figure 2.3).[18]

Figure 2.3. Sharing with a Point of View

Warrior is not alone. Richard Edelman, president and CEO of Edelman, the world's largest independently owned public relations firm, is another whose style of sharing packs a powerful punch. His blog posts get amplified, discussed, and passed around because he uses emotional appeal in the right doses and frequently shares a part of himself.[19] For example, he spoke with pride in one post: "Why I Joined My Father's Company," and then wrote in another post about a poignant moment at the 9/11 Memorial Museum in Lower Manhattan:[20]

> I was most profoundly affected by the small items in the gallery, much more than the crushed police car or charred ambulance. There was a pair of high heeled shoes with blood marks, worn by a woman who walked down the stairs before the buildings collapsed. There was a red bandana worn by a trader at a financial firm, a young former football player who went back to help colleagues escape by screening his mouth from the smoke and perished for his valor. There were

SHARE TO SHAPE   45

ephemera from the building, including legal documents and trading slips.

I asked Edelman why he shares the way he does—what value he sees being created for him and his firm. He responded, "It connects me with the people of Edelman and our clients in a personal way. It allows me to opine on topics in the PR industry, which very few of my fellow CEOs do ... I am going to the 70th anniversary of the Auschwitz-Birkenau liberation. I will meet survivors. I will also be in Davos. Why not share my experiences?"[21]

As Edelman and Warrior show, emotion hits people harder than facts and frameworks, and sharing that is done with humanity and a point of view gets noticed and amplified.

Sharing That's Memorable—Stories

Roger Martin, dean emeritus of the Rotman School of Management at the University of Toronto, writes in a blog post about the torturous process known as strategic planning.[22] Rather than approach planning as a series of constructed spreadsheets, he says, "Think about a strategic options [sic] as being just a happy story about the future." The best way to express and share a strategy is to show there's a beginning, a middle, and, most important, an end, as in a story. A story is memorable—people can remember it, talk about it, and articulate it. They might not remember the five points of a strategy, but they will remember the story behind it. The same holds true with sharing to shape. The more you can tie leadership to real stories or other memorable formats, the more people will remember, repeat, and adopt the ideas you are trying to convey. That's how shaping comes about.

Visuals Add Depth and Dimension to the Art of Sharing

It is possible that sharing to shape is in the water at Cisco, because CEO John Chambers seems to have the rules committed to memory as much as Warrior does. One of the most memorable videos from a top leader I've ever seen is one in which Chambers stands in his office in suit and tie, demonstrating duck calls with a series of successive whistles in perfect pitch.[23] One of his executives captured the scene with a Flip camera, and the rest is corporate history. It is a story that's told and retold, and the video was viewed 45,000 times on YouTube. Why would Chambers agree to do something like this? A quick look at the comments on the video reveals the video's impact—at least on a few Cisco employees (see Figure 2.4).

I'm not suggesting that all leaders get out their duck whistles and make a racket at the office. Instead, I am saying they should commit to sharing one story or memorable anecdote at a time in a way that will serve their purpose and help them shape relationships.

Figure 2.4. Comments from Cisco Employees Regarding CEO John Chambers Duck Call Video

Hi Jamisonft, You don't work in Cisco right? John, as a Leader is showing something very important via youtube. He is showing how different Cisco is from other companies regarding it's culture and vision. Cisco's Vision is "Changing the Way we Work, Live, Play and Learn". Hope you can learn with this because this is what makes Cisco so special. I'm proud of having John as my CEO. Thanks John, for this moment and for your vision in driving Cisco!

Our fearless leader has hidden talents we never knew about.

John Rocks!!! Multi talented, that's our leader!!!

Glad I work for a human being with interests outside of the corporate world instead of just another Wall St android!!!!! Thanks John, not only for the laughs, but for the sheer brilliance of guiding this company!!!!!

As the Chambers video illustrates, visuals introduce new dimension into the art of sharing. Seeing the Pope's selfies reprinted in *Vanity Fair*, for example, or watching Chambers quack online creates a much richer and potentially memorable experience than sharing with text exclusively. Text, pictures, videos—the art of sharing is a multimedia affair. Leaders need to use their judgment, but suffice it to say that a picture really is worth a thousand words and video is worth a thousand pictures. A well-crafted blog is fine, but photos and videos are easier and faster to produce.

Still, taking a picture and posting it may seem audacious to a leader who's more comfortable presenting a five-point plan. He may think, *Why would anyone be interested in this?* But let's say that he visits a key customer and she talks about how thrilled her organization is to be working with his. He could go back to the office and relay the positive news and hope it filters down to everyone involved. Or he could take a picture with that customer looking thrilled and giving a thumbs-up. *Here I am standing with our customer Jane. Jane is really happy. We're sitting in her office and she's giving me a thumbs-up. Great work, everybody!* That takes things to a higher level in terms of team building and engagement. You might even accompany the photo with a recording of Jane saying how much she loves the work everyone is doing. This type of thing creates an instant glow around the organization that a text message or simple conversation can never match.

The Science of Sharing

While the art of sharing to shape is all about *what* to share, the science described in this section is intended to clarify *how* to share. Such tools should simplify implementation in order to lessen the risk and restore predictability.

It's important to point out that sharing is simpler and (if done right) less time-consuming with the help of social and digital tools. Our vast connectivity means that it is just as possible to share with a workforce of 30,000 people as it is with a leadership team of 30. There are scheduling tools to enable posting at the proper hours across time zones, apps to abbreviate unwieldy links and condense lengthy files, and mobile platforms that make it a snap to share photos and other media, at any time and from any place. Yet even with the mobility that so many applications provide, thereby clearing the runway for sharing, many leaders need a framework to help them get started and become comfortable.

With that in mind, what follows are six implementation techniques to make sharing less messy and more manageable no matter what platform a leader chooses.

1. Create a Plan—Why? What? How?

When I talk with leaders and executives about sharing, they tend to go right to implementation questions such as *When should I use YouTube as opposed to Facebook?* This is a good query but nonetheless premature. Leaders need to begin by looping back to their objectives: What do you hope to take away from sharing and how does it connect to your overarching strategy? What relationships do you want to cultivate and why? Once you know why you are sharing, you can start to put together a content calendar for your audience and map it against social venues for sharing. Leaders like to have a plan, and this is a simple, linear starting point: 1. Goal (Why?), 2. Relationship (What?), 3. Venue (How?). Creating order around sharing helps leaders manage their time and create content strategically and with a larger purpose.

2. Curate Based on Listening

Sharing seldom requires creating all new content. If you're doing a good job of listening, you will be in a position to curate existing news and ideas and add your own perspective about why they are relevant. I tell leaders to start with messages and memes that already exist and add their own smart analysis. Ideas, research, and stories that your followers care about will come your way frequently. You can be the filter—decide what is sharable and portable. Similarly, retweeting on Twitter and reposting on LinkedIn or your blog are excellent ways to lend your perspective without becoming a full-time content creator.

3. Switch It Up

If you get stuck in the *idea* stage of what to share, try shifting your attention to the *medium*, and vice versa. You can publish a different version of the same content on a variety of platforms and it will look a little different every time—and reach a different audience to broaden your followership. Instagram features photos, Twitter allows 140 characters, and a video blog can be as long or as short as you'd like. This approach allows you to keep what you share fresh and still remain on message. Alternately, many leaders have a casual style that allows them to switch between business messaging and personal interests. Padmasree Warrior does this very well. She shares a little bit of everything and pulls it off because her point of view acts as the anchor and common denominator.

4. Schedule It

Besides having an authentic voice, Edelman PR CEO Richard Edelman is the iron man of executive blogging. He has been posting once a week for 10 years. You might think it comes naturally to the PR maven—and it might by now—but he got himself into it by creating a routine. Since September 2004 he has blogged, without fail, every single Tuesday morning at 6:00. He shared, "I almost never miss a week. I find something of interest somehow."[24] I coach leaders to set aside a small chunk of time regularly in order to write or plan content. Keep in reserve what you don't use so you have it when you need it. In the same way company announcements are scheduled, find a way to make a routine out of sharing.

One of my favorite routines is tweeting in advance. I use tools like TweetDeck, Hootsuite, and Buffer to binge-write tweets so they are queued up for a week to post at times when people are reading Twitter. I'll also schedule tweets to go out when I'm onstage giving a speech, as many of my audience members will be on Twitter during the event. These will be tweets that reinforce or extend my message. This way, I can amplify my message to a broader audience than the one in the room while also sharing content in a number of ways simultaneously.

5. Play to Your Strengths

One of the fundamental messages I have for top executives is that the transformation to digital leader should not take over their lives or overshadow the nature of their work. The job of a leader is to motivate others to act on behalf of the organization and provide them with inspiration and direction. Social and digital tools make that job easier—they don't replace it.

Contrary to what some would say, leaders needn't always be the ones to press "Send" when sharing. If they delegate some of the legwork—no problem. Bill Marriott, the executive chairman of Marriott, who is in his 80s, blogs all the time, despite the fact that he doesn't type. Sometimes he writes posts in long form, for example, during air travel, and then passes his notes to an assistant to post. Other times he sits in his office and dictates a

Figure 2.5. Blog Post from Marriott Executive Chairman Bill Marriott

IT ALL STARTED WITH A FORD MODEL T

January 11, 2015

It all started with a Ford Model T and a couple who had fallen in love. On the day they married, they left Salt Lake City, Utah and drove east until they hit Washington, D.C. The trip took 11 days. They went over a lot of hills, and the 'ol Ford Model T kept overheating. It was so tight in the cockpit that I have no idea how my parents sat comfortably in the front of that car. I guess they didn't sit comfortably. Do you know what air conditioning was back then? The AC was the window opening half way and praying for a gust of wind.

blog. He's not letting the fact that he doesn't type hold him back. He's the brains behind the operation, and that's what matters. Here's a recent post where he tells the story of how his parents drove a Model T across the country from Salt Lake City to Washington, DC, and started what eventually became Marriott (see Figure 2.5).

No one expects Michelle Obama to schedule tweets on her own. Sometimes she does, but more often it's a staffer posting on her behalf. As with everyone else, a leader's time is limited. Part of the point of mobile technology and social platforms is that they are easy to use anywhere, but that's not necessarily important for leaders. If someone else manages the password to their Hootsuite account, it does not necessarily diminish the quality of their sharing or the results of their efforts.

6. Be Intentional and Recalibrate

Before you share anything, think about how you will measure the return on your time investment. Knowing what kind of action you want to inspire, or what outlook you want to shape, needs to come first. Some people aspire to generate feedback, commentary, or retweets. Others want to gauge the traction their ideas are getting in the marketplace of ideas—and that type of concrete outcome is simple to measure. (Leave the job of tracking tweets and the pass-along rate to your social media team.) But the results that most leaders are looking for are more subjective. Changing minds and shaping behaviors over the long term is not an exact science. It's more like trial and error. Yet because the investment is relatively low, you can make a change when you are not getting the type of response you want. As with anything else, if one particular activity is not adding value, then you shouldn't be doing it. There are always trade-offs, so you need to give various approaches a try to see what will work for you in the digital world.

The Eye of the Beholder

Before moving on to the next chapter on engagement, it's important to acknowledge that not everyone will like everything you share. With 1.5 million Twitter followers, Cisco's Warrior is seen by most as dynamic and authentic. But occasionally,

Figure 2.6. Example Worksheet: Share to Shape

Goal	Attract and retain the best people in the industry.	Grow market share in our new target market.	Create an extraordinary experience for our customers.
Measurement	Improve retention rate to 90%.	Grow share to 25% of addressable market.	Increase customer satisfaction by 25%.
Listen at Scale	Look for ideas trending on internal digital platform.	Monitor the Twittersphere for ideas to serve the target market.	Listen (with your eyes) for trending—complaints and kudos on the company Facebook page.
Share to Shape	**Recognize high-achieving employees on internal social network.**	**Post videos about products and services, framed for the target market.**	**Tell a story of a customer encounter that reflects that extraordinary experience. Socialize it throughout the organization.**
Engage to Transform			

when I share Warrior's more personal posts, a few people react differently, and consider them inauthentic, as if she is trying too hard to be "real." I know Padmasree personally and see the authenticity behind every post she writes. But authenticity will always be in the eye of the beholder—you can be as authentic and transparent as you want, but you may not be *perceived* that way. You can't and likely won't please everyone. As you share, you will need to put yourself out there a bit and grow a tougher skin while making the transformation into an engaged leader. Sharing in a way that shapes and inspires action is a trial-and-error exercise that is worth the time and risk.

Let's take a moment to consider how you can share to shape strategic outcomes. Who would benefit from hearing from you? What stories would you want to share with them, and what actions would you like them to take as a result? Take the goals you identified from the introduction and think through how sharing could you help you accomplish those goals. Figure 2.6 uses the example goals as a starting point for some sharing initiatives.

Questions to Get Started

- What stories can you share to advance your top goals?
- What stories does your team/department/company/customer need to hear to develop affinity toward the organization?
- How will you know that your content has made a difference?
- What won't you share—what's off-limits?
- What tools (and help from others) will you use to enable your personal sharing?

CHAPTER 3

Engage to Transform

The CEO of the health-care giant Aetna threw the industry into chaos with a series of successive tweets. With one keystroke after another, Mark Bertolini dismantled the traditional rules of engagement assigned to CEOs: He reached out directly to an incensed policyholder via Twitter. He pointedly questioned the fundamentals of the managed-care business model. And he publicly agreed to override a cancer patient's policy parameters and pay every last penny of his considerable treatment costs.

The tweets that prompted Bertolini's response, and that touched off the firestorm of debate, came from Arizona State University graduate student Arijit Guha, who decried the inadequacy of his medical coverage and accused the industry and Bertolini himself of abandoning him in his hour of need. Guha was a young man with Stage IV colon cancer. After surgery and chemotherapy, the 30-year-old found that he had reached the $300,000 lifetime limit on his health coverage while additional medical bills were still piling up.[25] It was a public relations nightmare for Aetna and for Bertolini—whose salary at the time, including bonus, topped $10 million.

Bertolini could have turned a blind eye and left the situation to Aetna's army of legal and PR experts, but he chose to engage with Guha directly: "The system is broken and I am committed to fixing it," he tweeted.[26] "I am glad we connected today and got this issue solved. I appreciate the dialog no matter how pointed" (see Figure 3.1.).[27] The result: Aetna agreed to pay all Guha's

Figure 3.1. Mark Bertolini Engages Directly

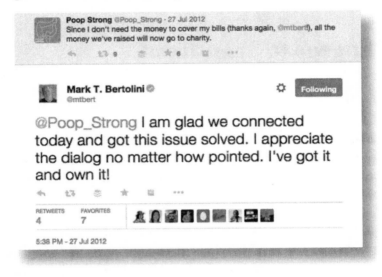

medical bills, and Bertolini's Twitter interaction was heralded as an example of enlightened social engagement.

Bertolini, a passionate advocate for health-care reform, is an engaged leader who felt comfortable jumping into the fray and engaging in a dialogue.[28] This wasn't the first time he had engaged with a patient or policyholder directly via digital channels, and it wasn't the only time he insisted that his industry could use a dramatic overhaul. But this engagement stood out for three reasons. First, Guha was insured by Arizona State University with Aetna as the underwriter, thereby making the situation notably complex in terms of relationships and business dynamics. Second, Guha's dramatic story was gaining considerable attention thanks to his personal appeal on Twitter—so this was a public relations issue as much as it was a point of policy.

Finally, Bertolini was potentially setting a precedent that he and Aetna would respond and capitulate to future patient demands made via social channels. The bottom line is that Bertolini took a risk by engaging, and it paid off. He established himself as an engaged leader and someone searching for innovative ways to improve health-care delivery. His style of engagement, although bold, was not haphazard. It directly and clearly correlated with his stated objectives and priorities. Therefore, it also improved his relationship with followers as opposed to creating distance or damage.

Why Engagement Transforms Leaders— and Their Organizations

When I talk to leaders about Bertolini's willingness to engage digitally, many share that they would have handled the crisis differently: *Make a promise like that to a customer one time and you open up the floodgates. Can he do that for every single patient? Bertolini's crazy for setting a precedent that he can't possibly adhere to.*

Yet Bertolini and leaders like him are privy to the immense upside of true digital engagement because they have experienced the benefits. When leaders engage with purpose, they achieve a transformation. In fact, engagement is the most powerful of the three steps described in this book because it differs most radically, in idea and practice, from our traditional notions of leadership. The first two steps—listening and sharing—are supporting platforms that make engagement a transformational tool for leaders (see Figure 3.2).

Before we dive into the mechanics of engaging to transform, let's take a moment to explore how listening and sharing come together to make engagement more potent.

Figure 3.2. Engage to Transform

Listening helps leaders see the context of a given issue more clearly and separate the signals from the noise. That way, they can get an accurate baseline assessment of which individuals and issues they should engage with. For example, Red Robin's latest menu item would not have been resuscitated if CEO Stephen Carley and his leadership team had not been tuned into the intelligence from restaurant servers. Once Red Robin executives were brought into the listening loop, they recognized that they needed to lean in even further to engage with front-line employees. Together they were able to rework their recipe and make the Pig Out Burger worthy of its audacious name.

Likewise, sharing puts employees and other stakeholders on the same page as leaders and gives them the direction they need to advance in lockstep. Rosemary Turner of UPS, we know, spends her days broadcasting across the company and sharing ideas and advice with thousands of employees. They hear her "voice" constantly, so when she reaches out to engage with a front-line colleague, he or she is fully prepared to step up and help solve whatever problem is at hand.

Both listening and sharing establish goodwill between leaders and followers and align people around common objectives. They strengthen relationships and pave the way for fruitful engagement between leaders and followers. Along with listening and sharing, engagement shapes relationships in a way that solidifies a leader's power and influence. But engagement is different and more powerful because it enables leaders to amass social capital. It is a very different type of social capital than leaders have established in the past, one that comes with being proactive and approachable.

Having an effective means to interact with followers enables leaders to improve and transform relationships like never before. Yet they need to do so carefully and intentionally. The fact that Bertolini decided to chime in personally, taking an interest in a critically ill patient, catapulted Aetna's response to the crisis to a totally new level. It was very mindful, very intentional of him to get involved, and the engagement paid off. You can bet that Bertolini's contact with Guha dramatically enhanced his standing with Aetna policyholders, health-care providers, and employees alike. Now more people than ever look at him and think, *This is a leader who really gets it.*

Changing Minds about Engagement

Engagement is where the biggest change happens on the road to becoming an engaged leader. Through digital means or otherwise, leaders need to listen to subordinates, customers, vendors, and others—they have no choice now. Sharing via digital channels, although perhaps more discretionary, has become more commonplace as well. Engagement in the digital age, however, is still a stretch for most leaders because it alters how they feel about themselves and how they normally act and it changes their relationships with followers.

Digital engagement is a complete paradigm shift that can be examined from three interrelated perspectives: distance, direction, and frequency.

Distance

Distance—or, more specifically, *power distance*—is the broadest way to examine how the digital age has altered engagement between leaders and the constellation of people surrounding them. The Dutch social psychologist Geert Hofstede used the term *power distance* to describe how a specific culture views relationship dynamics between people.[29] Individuals in cultures demonstrating a high power distance, according to Hofstede, are deferential to figures in authority and generally accept an unequal distribution of power, while individuals in cultures demonstrating a low power distance readily question authority and expect to participate in decisions that affect them. Intentionally reducing power distance is a key step in securing buy-in and participation in strategic initiatives—and it is a key reason leaders frequently engage in person by walking around and meeting people.

In the digital age, engagement greatly diminishes the power distance between leaders and subordinates because of the radical transparency of information and communications, social media, and wide-scale connectivity. Greater accessibility means being more open and transparent—and for some leaders, this comes with a sense of greater vulnerability. But for others it's a refreshing breath of fresh air because it allows them to step outside the bounds of formal hierarchies to develop authentic relationships. The decrease in power distance has a dramatic impact on who can engage with whom, for what reasons, and how often.

Direction

The decrease in power distance points right to the second way in which we can examine the shift in how leaders must engage–*direction*. The traditional rules of business engagement, borrowed from the military, are top down. Leaders determined the time, place, and nature of engagement. Rarely would somebody ever approach a leader with feedback or question his or her authority unless they were a close peer or the leader's boss. But today people at all levels initiate digital engagement, asking leaders about their plans, goals, decisions, and mandates, across the entire spectrum of the organization and industry. With digital and social tools, hierarchy and the chain of command disappear and the rules of engagement become less formal—and, some would argue, more confusing—with each passing day.

Frequency

The third way to examine the shift created by digital engagement is by looking at *frequency*. Although leaders can decide how often they engage, they can't stem the constant tide of requests that flow in from above, below, and beyond. They have to expect that people, both internally and externally, will reach out 24/7 simply because they have the means to do so. This increased frequency of engagement is a challenge to leaders in a number of ways, most notably because they can't meet outsize expectations to be available to respond. Just thinking about the potential burden in terms of time and attention is enough to dissuade leaders from even considering engaging digitally.

Reduced power distance, change in direction, and increase in frequency mean that leaders are no longer insulated. They are not the protected species they once were. And yet with all this newness come tremendous benefits and opportunities. It is an opportunity for engaged leaders to transform the entire organization through their engagement—with one person at a time or everyone at once. Leadership means constantly reinforcing the direction an organization is taking, and engagement opens up new and better ways to steer business transformation.

Digital Engagement Strategy: Art and Science Overlap

Many leaders shy away from direct digital engagement because of the slew of changes and challenges just mentioned. To face these challenges, it is important that leaders have a *digital engagement strategy* to inform their interactions and add a layer of transparency. This strategy, described in the following box, integrates art and science in an action plan divided into four elements. The art side is focused on engaging followers in a way that suits each leader's goals and leadership style. The science side is intended to make digital leadership more predictable and manageable. With practice, persistence, and a plan, leaders can go from being introverted in how they engage, staying within their comfortable circle of peers, to more extroverted in how they reach out and interact with followers.

Digital Engagement Strategy

> **Art: qualitative measures**
> 1. Choose the right type of engagement.
> 2. Cultivate followership.
>
> **Science: quantitative measures**
> 3. Define the end result of engagement.
> 4. Put controls in place.

Art—Engaging to Cultivate Relationships

The art part of our engagement strategy focuses on the relationship one hopes to build and on *qualitative* outcomes as they relate to specific interactions. We will start by looking at which type of engagements leaders might choose from and then will consider how a leader wants the engagement to affect followers.

Choose the Right Type of Engagement

The fact of the matter is that people want to engage with leaders a lot more frequently than leaders want to (or can) engage with them. That's where the tension around an engagement strategy comes in. Leaders fear engagement because they're convinced they may not have all the answers their followers need. More than that, they are concerned about managing their limited time and bandwidth.

Yet this is the allure of engagement in the digital era. Like sharing, engagement can happen at scale (one to many) and still leave followers with the sense of access to leaders that they are looking for—and that's empowering. It used to be a really big deal for the CEO to show up at the call center and say, "I'll sit down next to you and join the call, okay?" Employees might have fidgeted in their seats, but they felt special. Now leaders can do something like that anytime, right from their desk if they so desire—if that's the type of engagement they believe will make a difference.

In terms of an engagement strategy, understanding some types and levels of engagement will help leaders determine which may suit their particular needs. There is an art to determining which is right for you, but it begins with educating yourself. There are any number of ways to engage, but here are three that demonstrate the variety of engagement possibilities, along with advice on how to get started with each type.

1. Event-Based Engagement

Event-based engagement is where leaders make themselves available in an open-forum setting at a particular time and place. It's an extension of a familiar format that leaders are largely comfortable with—but with a social and digital twist. This type of engagement might be akin to the "Ask Me Anything" sessions online where leaders, as well as experts and celebrities, answer questions posted by public participants. Or it might look like a live corporate town hall meeting where employees in multiple locations watch on a screen and submit their comments and questions digitally.

An event-based engagement is more impactful when executives use it to engage at scale. Humana CEO and president Bruce Broussard, for example, started engaging employees as a regular contributor on the organization's internal platform. Originally he used the platform as a focus group mechanism to test ideas. Now he uses it to host monthly meetings with top executives. He also hosts larger quarterly meetings where 6,000 Humana leaders ask questions and network. Broussard makes content from these sessions public within a few days of the meeting, and 55,000 Humana employees can participate in the ongoing conversation. These forums are widely anticipated by the general population at Humana and are considered to be extremely successful in terms of the engagement they create. In this company's case, the key success factor was providing open access to senior leaders in a structured way. Leaders are willing to discuss anything employees throw at them.

An event-based engagement can be large in scale, but it is also relatively controlled—the time span is limited, the content is often organized by topic, and the circumstances are managed. The multimedia requirements of an event-based engagement can add a level of complexity. Nonetheless, such events are an easy starting point for those who are accustomed to engaging with live audiences.

2. Participatory Engagement

Participatory engagement invites people to answer a particular question, comment on a post, or establish a priority. Engaging within this context puts followers at ease because it levels the playing field, in that everyone's opinion matters equally. The engagement is similar to that provided by a feedback survey, but the simple fact that the leader is asking the question from his account implies that he is not only involved but also personally interested in each person's response. Who wouldn't want to bend the ear of an executive, especially when you know he is interested, listening, and ready to take action?

We saw in Chapter 1 how David Thodey, CEO of Telstra, the largest telecommunications company in Australia, listens actively to what is happening inside the company with an enterprise social network from Yammer. While Thodey will tell you that he is still on a journey to learn how to be an engaged leader, I consider him one of the masters, especially when it comes to engagement. Here's an example of him using participatory engagement, where he extends listening with engagement to reinforce to employees that he is interested in their thoughts and concerns and that they all need to work in concert. At one point he asked the entire company, "What processes and technologies should we eliminate?" The question received more than 830 responses and gave Thodey an intimate look into what wasn't working at Telstra (see Figure 3.3). And to show that he was doing more than just listening, Thodey put many of the suggestions into practice.

The key success factor for participatory engagement is follow-through—once you've gathered the input and feedback, what will you do with it? Thodey charged his team with systematically reviewing and analyzing the hundreds of responses. They made

Figure 3.3. Engagement at Telstra

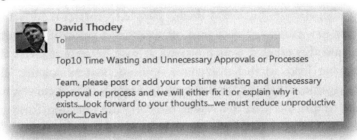

David Thodey
To

Top10 Time Wasting and Unnecessary Approvals or Processes

Team, please post or add your top time wasting and unnecessary approval or process and we will either fix it or explain why it exists...look forward to your thoughts...we must reduce unproductive work....David

visible changes to processes as a result. By being responsive and closing the loop, Thodey sent a message that employee participation made a difference. Employees are smart—they won't waste their time on stunts that are purely for show. Use participatory engagement to involve employees in making decisions that matter.

3. Personal Engagement

Looking toward the other end of the spectrum, personal engagements are one-on-one interactions that happen using tools such as internal social networks, public social media accounts, or even email. As we just saw, Mark Bertolini connected with Arijit Guha directly and personally, and it became a public interaction. But more often, personal engagements are quiet opportunities for leaders to strengthen a particular relationship by repairing a rift or thanking someone for his or her service.

At Telstra, Thodey uses the company's internal social network to reach out directly to individual employees, and he uses Twitter and LinkedIn to engage with individuals outside Telstra. For example, here is Thodey engaging with a less-than-happy customer on Twitter (see Figure 3.4).[30]

Figure 3.4. David Thodey's Personal Engagement

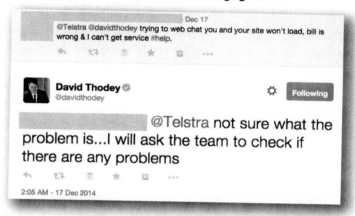

> Dec 17
>
> @Telstra @davidthodey trying to web chat you and your site won't load, bill is wrong & I can't get service #help.

David Thodey ✔
@davidthodey   Following

@Telstra not sure what the problem is...I will ask the team to check if there are any problems

2:05 AM - 17 Dec 2014

Thodey makes it look easy, mostly because he comes to this with a background in anthropology (as an undergrad in college) and a natural disposition to engage. But the reality is that personal external engagement is something that Thodey approaches with great care and a lot of advance planning. He is concerned primarily about his ability to consistently engage with customers, and he doesn't want to set expectations that he can't meet. His solution is having backup—a member of Thodey's communications team scans Twitter and alerts him to any issues that require his attention. Then it's up to him to decide when and how to engage and respond, which he does personally.

Initially, Thodey was concerned that the time spent engaging would be all-consuming, but when I asked him how he manages to keep up, his response was telling. He shrugged and said, "I jump into customer issues because it's dear to my heart." If someone takes the time to reach out to him directly, he explained, it usually means that person has exhausted all other avenues for resolution. With this type of customer contact connected to a strategic goal, Thodey finds interstitial time to flick through Twitter or take a spin through Yammer. He reflected, "People overestimate how much time it takes, but it's really just a few minutes here and there."

Thodey aside, many leaders find personal engagement difficult because it is personal, potentially time-consuming, and requires a high-touch approach. I am not suggesting that every leader engage personally in digital channels—especially if they are not ready for it. Depending on goals and personality, it is not the right approach for every leader. What I *do* suggest is that leaders be *intentional* about deciding if and how they will personally engage, rather than do nothing by default. I have enormous respect for someone like Ginni Rometty, who has made a conscious decision to abstain from a platform like Twitter because it doesn't align with her strategic goals.

As we've seen, some types of engagements are proactive while others are reactive; some require enormous psychic effort while others are essentially automated. Part of the art of digital leadership is deciding which types of engagement to use and when. It all depends on what action or feeling you expect the interaction to inspire in followers.

Cultivate Followership—How You Will Make Followers Think, Feel, or Act

Part of the art in an engagement strategy centers on the relationship one hopes to build with followers, a practice referred to by some business scholars as "followership."[31] For our purposes the focus is on how digital engagement encourages employees to assert their independence of thought and action while remaining united in the pursuit of strategic goals. Focusing on how followers think and feel results in positive qualitative outcomes such as increasing trust and credibility. This is often perceived as the "softer" side of engagement, but make no mistake—mastering followership requires laserlike focus on outcomes. In some cases you may design an engagement to deliver a sense of familiarity and accessibility, while in other situations you will want to instill a sense of confidence perhaps, or even authority and control. With each interaction, frame your mode of engagement accordingly. Simply keeping in mind the type of relationship you want to develop will help you choose and design engagements that cultivate followers.

David Thodey shared a keen insight with me, saying, "Organizations are nothing more than a community of people coming together to hopefully achieve something bigger than what they could individually." Taking a page from classic community management, he employs techniques to develop a specific type of feeling and outcome with each engagement. For example, in Figure 3.5, Thodey responds to a problem brought to the surface by an employee on the internal social network.

Thodey's brief interaction is managed with precision. First he empathizes with the employee's situation. Then he pulls in people who can be part of a solution. The result Thodey is going for is to make the employee feel heard and valued. His problem is being taken seriously. And with digital engagement comes a multiplier effect. Because the conversation is seen potentially by every employee (or, in the case of external platforms like Twitter and LinkedIn, by a much larger audience), other people will experience the same effect through engagement by proxy. Individuals across the organization and beyond begin to see that Thodey and his leaders are engaged, and this starts to change relationships for the better.

Figure 3.5. Thodey and the Art of Followership

In online community management, moderators of venues such as Sephora's BeautyTalk or the technical community Spiceworks understand the power of every interaction and the impact each has on the community. Likewise, corporate leaders need to think through how each engagement adds up to achieve their goals. One key element to consider is how to use language within the engagements themselves. Rachel Happe at The Community Roundtable shared a keen insight in a recent post, writing, "In most business communications the emphasis is on being declarative and crafting a well thought-out and complete thought ... But the enemy of engagement is perfection. The more complete your thought, the less other opinions and input is [sic] needed. Complete and perfect communications are a transaction, not a conversation."[32]

Happe's takeaway is that engagement must be interactive. It is an imperfect dialogue that changes and evolves. Be aware, too, that engagement takes time. Also, in the beginning, it often

---

Language for Cultivating Followership

The voice you use to engage followers depends in part on your goals and intent. Sometimes leaders need to take an authoritative tone, especially when stating a clear direction or opinion. Other times leaders need to strike a difficult balance, with a voice that is modest, imperfect, and human while not coming across as passive or solicitous. It's in this second area where leaders sometimes struggle.

The Community Roundtable's Rachel Happe offers these best practices from community management that leaders can employ to develop followership:[33]

- Be careful about using absolutes—*always, never, no, yes*
- When expressing an opinion (which is important to do because differences are where innovation and change come from), use phrases like "in my experience", "I have found", "I think", and "from my perspective," which allow an opening for them and encourages them to share their experiences and perspectives.
- Use *but* and *should* sparingly. *But* arrests a conversation and takes it in a different direction, implicitly judging another comment as incomplete or misdirected. *Should* is often used when you are telling someone what you think he ought to do, which is a dynamic of control versus engagement.
- Use *you* and *we* carefully for similar reasons—both words can subtly indicate control over ideas and people.
- Be curious and ask a lot of questions, even if you think someone's issue has been addressed. There is often more to the story, and this kind of probing can lead to better understanding and, sometimes, a different answer.

looks and feels like awkward teenage dating. No one knows what this new relationship is about, and the rules are unclear. When the Accounts Payable intern is riding alone in an elevator with the CEO, for example, he's afraid to open his mouth and say the wrong thing. But it's arguably worse for the CEO—she feels awkward when a 23-year-old employee comments on the company's latest missteps. It's uncomfortable for everyone, and it takes some getting used to. It requires openness, honesty, and even, at times, vulnerability. This is something that Thodey honed through trial and error in the relative safety of Telstra's internal social network.

Figure 3.6 shows an engagement in the comments to one of Thodey's recent posts on LinkedIn that illustrates the type of humility combined with confidence and resolve that takes time and experience to develop.[34]

Science—Managing Goals and Controls

Like many of the rules of engagement we have explored, the science side of engagement is intended to make digital transformation more predictable and manageable. In order to achieve that outcome, a leader can focus on two things: goals and controls.

Define the Goals of Engagement

As stated throughout this book, defining your goals, and using those goals as the basis for your engagement strategy, is a critical part of planning to engage. When digital engagement is connected to long-term goals from the outset, it will move your leadership agenda forward faster. It is a way not only to achieve those long-term goals but also to align the organization behind addressing critical issues and problems.

Figure 3.6. Thodey Engages and Responds to Criticism

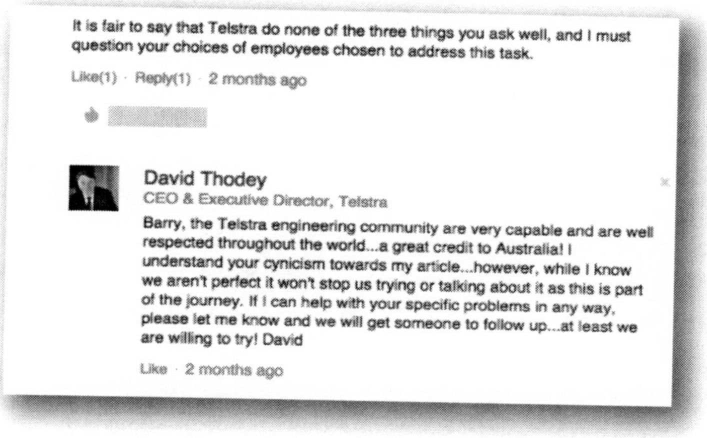

> It is fair to say that Telstra do none of the three things you ask well, and I must question your choices of employees chosen to address this task.
>
> Like(1) · Reply(1) · 2 months ago
>
> **David Thodey**
> CEO & Executive Director, Telstra
>
> Barry, the Telstra engineering community are very capable and are well respected throughout the world...a great credit to Australia! I understand your cynicism towards my article...however, while I know we aren't perfect it won't stop us trying or talking about it as this is part of the journey. If I can help with your specific problems in any way, please let me know and we will get someone to follow up...at least we are willing to try! David
>
> Like · 2 months ago

At Telstra, David Thodey uses social media to engage, very intentionally, with two specific goals in mind. The first is to achieve a better understanding of what's going on across the company. According to Thodey, "One of the biggest challenges of leadership is getting the unadulterated truth and understanding the reality of what is happening in the business."[35] This goes beyond simply listening to what employees and customers are saying and doing—he uses engagement to dig deeper.

He's always looped in, and the result is that people see he's deeply interested in the work they're doing. He has his finger on the pulse of everything going on at Telstra, and it puts him in a great position to shape the organization one day at a time. Along the same lines, Thodey recently went on Yammer rather than using management consultants to define the characteristics of an "ideal Telstra leader." More than 700 responses later, feedback on traits such as *caring, passionate,* and *committed* are being highlighted in development plans across the business.

The second goal Thodey has in mind when using social media to engage is more strategic—he wants the entire 40,000+ organization to pivot toward being more present and connected to the customer experience. How is he planning to accomplish that goal? By changing the culture across the company. "My goal is to create a culture that is open and transparent," Thodey shared. "Transparency creates accountability, and individuals can opt in to make a difference." He went on to say, "You get that in a start-up company, but in big organizations the default is conformity and a lack of accountability. The fear factor of speaking up is a real issue."[36]

Thodey's resolve was put to the test in August 2014, when the company announced internally that it had missed its customer service targets and would not be paying out full annual bonuses as a result. Employees were indignant that they would not be getting the part of their bonus based on customer service goals. In many cases, including senior leadership, this figure was as high as 40% of overall bonuses.

While discussions on Telstra's Yammer network are usually balanced, this time the chatter was entirely negative, and quite blunt, even for Australians. But Thodey didn't whitewash the situation. Instead, he saw an opening and jumped in with his own perspective, writing, "I don't like it either. I'm disappointed, but the numbers are the numbers and we missed our goal."[37] Thodey, they learned, wasn't receiving a customer service bonus either. The impact was immediate—employees didn't expect their CEO to lose the bonus right along with them. Although they were still unhappy with the outcome, people began to accept the rationale for the decision and the importance of making customer service the centerpiece of their work.

As an aspiring engaged leader, consider how engaging directly and personally can help you achieve your strategic goals.

This is where the art is—each leader must identify and articulate what goals are most important to him or her. When leaders engage with their goals in mind, it helps them prioritize efforts while keeping the entire organization focused on what matters.

Put Controls in Place

The second way to practice the science of engagement is to put key controls in place. Many leaders are reluctant to engage because they fear that it's tantamount to opening up Pandora's box. But in reality it can mean exactly the opposite. Engagement is something that leaders themselves should command. A vitally important component of digital leadership is creating rules of engagement for oneself that are sustainable. You choose what, when, and with whom to engage. Start with your specific goals and then build the controls around them in the following three ways.

1. Set Expectations

There's no one right way to engage; it's wide open. Real-time engagement versus programmed; periodic versus frequent interaction; chief executives leading the charge personally versus a team effort—the key is that it is the leader's engagement to define and design.

Telstra's David Thodey, for instance, engages frequently across multiple platforms, internally and externally. He feels comfortable talking about everything—work, family, hobbies, and so on. Thodey is open and constantly engaging. Ginni Rometty of IBM has different rules of engagement. Most people know little about her private life because she never talks about herself. It's all business with Rometty, and she keeps her engagements clearly focused. Bruce Broussard, CEO of Humana, falls somewhere in the middle.

He is an active contributor on Humana's internal platforms and recently started posting on Twitter. He also hosts the monthly town hall session with Humana's 40,000 employees. But it's never a free-for-all. Broussard and other company executives discuss anything employees ask—but it is a once-a-month engagement with specified start and end times.

In August 2012, President Obama enhanced his street cred when he agreed to be the guest of an "Ask Me Anything" session on Reddit, making himself the first sitting president to participate in the Wiki-style news site's popular Q&A feature.[38] However, his credibility was knocked down half a peg when he failed to address the most frequently asked question—regarding the legalization of marijuana and the role the federal government plays in enforcing drug laws. The nature of the AMA format set up openness expectations that Obama, however well intentioned, couldn't possibly meet. The lesson here is to set clear expectations and guidelines at the onset and choose your formats for engaging accordingly. In Obama's case, he could have stated up front that he would skip certain topics. Alternatively, he could have avoided the AMA format altogether and chosen a venue that suited his needs as a leader.

2. Set Limits

The toughest part of the science of engagement is triage. To whom and about what will you engage? Topics come up quickly and demand a commensurate response. The simple way to break it down and make it all manageable is to create a playbook that specifies how you will engage, with whom, and under what circumstances. List the topics, venues, and time frames. Make sure your extended team understands the playbook, and revise it whenever needed. The Telstra communications and social media team, for instance, meticulously planned their playbook, encompassing each type and level of engagement for their CEO—and they continually revised it with his input. Being an engaged leader requires instinct and savvy, to be sure, but having a reference tool removes some of the guesswork for you and everyone on the team.

3. Determine What to Delegate

Digital engagement is not something most leaders should do entirely on their own. Relying on your team to pick up the slack is the strategic way to engage. With that in mind, determine what you want to delegate to your staff and include this in the playbook so it is clear who's running point on each issue and relationship. Decide what goes on the overall dashboard and think about each concurrent level of engagement—your own as well as engagements moderated by your team.

It is important to determine up front how much of the engaging you will do personally versus how much you will delegate to your team. Telstra's David Thodey does all his own posting, something he insisted on from the start. His logic: "I sign all of my own letters, and I want people to know that I personally stand behind every post." But he does get help from his team—they may contribute to drafting a longer-form blog post for LinkedIn, or identify topics for him to post on, but Thodey insists on pushing the Submit button on everything.

The vast majority of leaders do and should rely on their teams for help. They may direct the content and tone, and approve topics and posts, but they should leave the mechanics to someone else. There is no right way to proceed, but again, ask what kind of relationship and outcomes you want to achieve, and how delegation will help, or hinder, your ability to achieve those results.

Getting Started with Engagement

Engaging to transform is the capstone step in the journey to becoming an engaged leader. It involves listening and sharing (both are integral parts of engagement) and interacting with

Figure 3.7. Example Worksheet: Engage to Transform

Goal	Attract and retain the best people in the industry.	Grow market share in our new target market.	Create an extraordinary experience for our customers.
Measurement	Improve retention rate to 90%.	Grow share to 25% of addressable market.	Increase customer satisfaction by 25%.
Listen at Scale	Look for ideas trending on internal digital platform.	Monitor the Twittersphere for ideas to serve the target market.	Listen (with your eyes) for trending—complaints and kudos on the company Facebook page.
Share to Shape	Recognize high-achieving employees on internal social network.	Post videos about products and services, framed for the target market.	Tell a story of a customer encounter that reflects that extraordinary experience. Socialize it throughout the organization.
Engage to Transform	Host "Ask Me Anything" sessions on internal digital platform.	Solicit suggestions from front-line employees on improving the company's offerings and then follow through.	Selectively connect with customers directly on social media to solve problems.

followers in a thoughtful way either at scale or one to one. Engagement creates a natural continuum. In the process, it aligns people around common objectives. And just as important, engagement fosters key relationships. This is part of what makes engagement precious—it has tremendous meaning for the people with whom a leader chooses to engage. It is a tool, therefore, that should be used wisely and intentionally. If it becomes commonplace, it may lose its value.

Round out your engaged leader strategic plan by identifying how and when you will engage to transform relationships. Go back to the strategic goals identified in the introduction and think through how engagement can help you achieve those objectives. Note that you may choose not to engage. If that is the course you take, be thoughtful and intentional about deciding and balance it with strong listening and sharing activities. Figure 3.7 provides an example of how engagement could support the sample goals we identified.

Questions to Get Started

- When will you engage—and how will the engagement move the relationship forward?
- How will your engagement develop and deepen the relationship with your customers, employees, partners, and investors?
- How will you actively maintain the relationship with your followers?
- How will you manage and scale engagement?

CHAPTER 4

Transform the Organization

A number of years back, I was chatting with GE CEO Jeffrey Immelt when he noted that he wasn't on social media because, as he said, "That's the CMO's job."[39] At the time, that may have been true. CEOs were seldom on Twitter prior to 2010, and few organizations had broadly adopted social and mobile tools—those were the early days of digital media. It took time, but today Immelt is rooted in social technology. He joined Twitter in 2012, and he tweets with regularity and from a personal perspective (see Figure 4.1).[40] He also writes an internal blog that is widely read across GE. Launched in 2011 as a means of

---

Figure 4.1. Tweet from GE CEO Jeffrey Immelt

reaching out to the nearly 300,000 GE employees worldwide, Immelt's "On My Mind" blog has been an ideal venue for sharing his observations.

One of the things that has struck me as I've watched Immelt's transformation into an engaged leader is that he has made the move gradually and in increments that suit his personal style. In 2010, when he was asked to deliver the commencement speech at Boston College, for example, he sent an email to a subset of GE employees to solicit their ideas for what topics to include in the speech. Of all the ways one might crowdsource a commencement speech, email may have seemed old school compared to Wiki technology and other social platforms. But email was what he was comfortable with at the time. And it worked beautifully—Immelt received hundreds of email responses from GE employees, and a number of those made their way into his speech.[41]

Becoming an engaged leader is a personal journey, and bona fide transformation doesn't happen in a day. And just as leadership styles vary greatly, no two approaches are exactly alike. There are a number of reasons CEOs make the difficult journey, but most times it is because they catch a glimpse of the incredible upside in terms of achieving their goals more effectively.

For example, Carolyn Miles, CEO of the international NGO Save the Children, came to social media because she had a clear goal—to mobilize support and provide critical help and relief to fight health crises affecting children, such as the Ebola outbreak in West Africa that came to a head in 2014. When she became CEO of Save the Children in 2011, the organization was already active in social media. Senior management discussed if it made sense for her to be active as well, and how it would help the organization. Miles recalled, "We decided it was important

Figure 4.2. Tweet from Save the Children CEO Carolyn Miles

Carolyn Miles @carolynsave · Jan 21
With r Board member Debra Fine in #Guatemala - no matter where you go, kids love 2 see themselves on camera #sweet

for audiences to know there are real people behind Save the Children, and not just institutional accounts."[42] She began writing a blog (called "Logging Miles"), posting on *Huffington Post*, and using Twitter.[43] Her content is packed with stories and photos that appeal to donors at a grassroots level (see Figure 4.2).[44] For Miles, engaging in social channels was an open-and-shut case. It suited her needs perfectly. In other instances, leaders need additional time and space to be persuaded to make the leap.

Change Is a Process

When Mike Smith, CEO of the Australia and New Zealand Banking Group (ANZ), was invited to publish a regular blog on LinkedIn's "Influencer" platform in 2013, it was reported on the front page of Australia's major business newspaper as breaking news.[45] Slow news day? Perhaps, but as Smith himself has said, "it showed how novel it was for CEOs to embrace a presence on social media" (see Figure 4.3).[46]

Figure 4.3. LinkedIn Post from ANZ CEO Mike Smith

Mike Smith [in]fluencer
Chief Executive Officer at ANZ

Following

How I became a social media believer and why banking's future is digital

Apr 14, 2014   16,866   351   49

I joined LinkedIn's influencer program last year and it was reported on the front page of Australia's major business newspaper as breaking news. Front page? Perhaps it showed how novel it was for CEOs to embrace a presence on social media.

Although something of a digital evangelist now, Smith admits that he harbored doubts for years about engaging in digital channels. And he's not alone. The journey to becoming an engaged leader is a change process like any other, and it unfolds in stages. Most leaders are familiar with the Kübler-Ross model—the series of emotional stages individuals face following a dramatic loss, such as that of a loved one, commonly called the five stages of grief. The stages have been adapted in a wide array of other settings to explain the emotions associated with accepting other types of major change.

For many leaders, for instance, the move to digital leadership is akin to a loss. Their old understanding of leadership, including what is expected of them, has undergone a shift, and it is a challenge to accept the new, altered vision of reality. Power structures have changed, and control has been disbursed across the organization. Recognizing the stages in this transformation of modern leadership delivers two benefits. First, it can help leaders understand what they are feeling, thereby hastening the journey to acceptance and transformation. Second, it can enable leaders at every level of an organization to become change agents and encourage others to embrace the future. I've adapted the Kübler-Ross model and boiled it down for our purposes to four stages:

Stage One: Denial (Anger, Dismissal, Repudiation)

Leaders stuck in the denial stage of the journey will look upon digital, mobile, and social platforms purely as fads. They may insist that they are *not going to fall for it*. Depending on the culture of an organization, deniers may be numerous, and there might even be social capital to be earned by being a technology naysayer. Further, they may believe *If I can outlast the bright shiny object of the moment, once it fades, I can keep doing what I am doing.* Deniers won't engage in much discussion about digital, and instead will dismiss it with one-liners such as "What could I possibly say in 140 characters that is meaningful?" Finally, individuals in the denial state will often virtually pat change evangelizers on the head, treating them as if they were suffering from a passing delusion, and think, *Don't worry, you'll come to your senses soon!*

Stage Two: Bargaining (Excuses, Escape, Desperation)

Bargainers see that they are running out of time fast and are looking for an escape hatch. They might be in numerous company. If so, they will form a "last stand" coalition to lobby against the change. In addition, bargainers will ask themselves (and others), *What can I say or do that will change their minds? How open do I need to be? How little can I change?* For a top-level leader, the common bargaining stance will be *Can I get my communications team to do this for me? Can I delegate this to the marketers? Isn't this a job for the social media team?*

Stage Three: Acceptance (Agreement, Realization, Awakening)

Acceptance occurs, and suddenly leaders acknowledge that maybe digital has some legs. They accept that it has taken off within their industry or organization and they log in or register for an account. At first they may be going through the motions, getting their feet wet, but then they realize, *This is something that works.* The light finally turns green in the acceptance phase, and leaders catch a glimpse of the full upside of digital engagement.

ANZ's Mike Smith's personal journey to acceptance took a major leap forward when he realized that being digital is not about technology or "being up to date with the latest thing." Instead, he came to realize "It's part of the focus business needs to have on being customer-centric by engaging customers and improving their experience with us."[47] That is when Smith's eyes opened to the potential of embracing digital leadership.

Stage Four: Transformation (Belief, Embracement, Evangelization)

The transformation stage is in sight when you move from tentatively exploring social and digital solutions because you have to, to embracing them because you believe they represent important new ways to be innovative and achieve your goals. Both your energy level and idea flow increase as you see a new world of potential and possibilities. Following his transformation, Smith became an active Influencer on LinkedIn and started ANZ BlueNotes, an independent content site covering the financial markets, on which he is a frequent contributor.

The key to expediting the journey is recognizing which stage you are in. And when you are supporting other leaders in their transformation, respect where they are in their journeys. Provide them with the time, space, and support they need to move smoothly through the change process.

Transforming the Organization

Much of this book has been dedicated to unpacking and assembling an implementation framework—listen, share, and engage. It provides a structure to facilitate your personal digital transformation. As that occurs, you will need to be ready to help the other leaders around you reach the acceptance stage and transform their thinking as well. Whether you are a top leader preparing to change the culture within your company, a unit leader charged with engaging a cohort of managers, or a front-line leader working to funnel ideas and innovation up through the organization, there are a number of things you can do to help hasten the transformation.

We will look at this by job level, but keep in mind that the advice offered for each is not exclusive to that level. Ideally, you can treat the prescriptions here as à la carte, picking and choosing as you like to put a plan in place to foster digital transformations in your organization.

Managing Up: When the Executive Is in Denial

It is not uncommon for CEOs and other top leaders to arrive fashionably late to the party. Selling your big boss on digital transformation requires less rather than more. First, stick to the big picture. Talk to her about what social and digital tools can accomplish for her, not what any particularly cool technology does. (Otherwise she will understand what Twitter does, for example, but not what it can accomplish for her in particular.) Here are some examples of how social business drives business impact across the organization (see Figure 4.4).

Next, start small. Choose one area of the business or one domain and explain how it can be improved. Let her draw her own conclusions about transforming the larger organization. Finally, emphasize ways to wade into using digital tools that doesn't require a major time commitment. Part of this entails exploring what she will *not* need to do anymore as a result of the efficiencies and scale of digital and social tools.

Managing in the Middle: Bringing Middle Managers on Board

Middle managers can be one of the most difficult groups to bring along because digital and social tools can feel like a threat to their authority. First, they see direct reports circumventing the established chain of command and reaching out directly to top executives. Likewise, executives via social tools are going around them to try to find out what "really" is going on in the

Figure 4.4. Business Impact of Social Business

Marketing and Sales	Customer Service	Innovation	Operations and Business Support
Derive Customer Insights	Provide Customer Care via Social Channels	Faster & Better Collaboration with Teams	Leverage Social Data to Forecast Demand through the Supply Chain
Use Social Media for Customer Interactions	Anticipate Problems in Advance via Insights	Surface Ideas from Across the Organization	Streamline Business Processes Such as Financial Closes
Generate and Foster Sales Leads	Enable Customer-to-Customer Support	Co-Create Products with Customers	Use Social Data to Match Talent to Task

organization. This leaves midlevel leaders feeling out of sorts and out of the loop. The traditional definition of a middle manager is to act as a gatekeeper—passing information up and decisions down. Yet as social networks improve communication and reduce the power distance in the organization, this gatekeeper role isn't needed.

Second, middle managers aspire to move up into top leadership positions, but digital is transforming those roles as well—creating confusion around promotion paths. Given their discomfort with digital engagement, midlevel leaders don't have as many opportunities to develop digital leadership skills. Without focused intervention, they are apt to get stuck in the denial or bargaining stages.

The key to getting them unstuck is to redefine what it means to be a middle manager. Rather than being gatekeepers, they become facilitators. They listen, share, and engage at multiple levels throughout and across the organization, breaking down silos and identifying barriers to action. By shifting their role, they are made indispensable rather than extraneous. In essence, hastening their journey to acceptance and digital transformation requires showing them what is in it not just for the organization, but also for them.

Taking It from the Top: Managing from the C-Suite

If your organization is so lucky as to have transformed leaders who fully embrace and engage in digital and social channels, don't take it for granted! All too often I see these leaders happily engaging individually but not actively and intentionally developing other leaders in the organization. Here are a few things that leaders can do to foster and support digital leadership.

- **Clarify goals and objectives.** After taking the leap themselves, CEOs and other top executives will have some work to do in encouraging others to follow in their footsteps. The best thing any leader can do is to socialize her digital agenda, customize if needed, so that everyone is executing from the same playbook. Starting with your end goals in mind has been a common refrain throughout this book, and it becomes even more vital when bringing others into the loop for implementation. This means clearly delineating not only goals but also boundaries, so that line leaders can see how the organization expects digital to be integrated into their work.

- **Set the tone.** Top leaders are accustomed to setting the tone for their organization on big-picture strategy and goals, and digital transformation is no exception. If top leaders are social in a digital sense, then that sensibility trickles down. As always, leaders look up to see what cues they can take from the top.

• **Invest in formal training.** Creating time and space for training is the other important ingredient for increasing a leader's comfort with digital leadership at every level. Our research and executive advisory work at Altimeter has found that training needs to be more than assigning a reverse mentor

---

Figure 4.5. Worksheet: Digital Leadership Development

Step 1: Goals
List up to three strategic goals and how you plan to measure their achievement.

Step 2: Listen at Scale
Describe who or what you need to listen to in order to accomplish each of your goals. Be specific. If you need tools, resources, or training to listen at scale, list them here.

Step 3: Share to Shape
Describe what you will share—and what you won't—in order to achieve your goals. What stories can you tell that will inspire action? If you need tools, resources, or training to share to shape, list them here.

Step 4: Engage to Transform
Describe when, with whom, and how you intend to engage and respond. How will engagement develop and deepen the relationship? If you need tools, resources, or training to engage to transform, list them here.

Step 5: Create Your Engaged Leader Strategic Plan
Gather the information from the previous step and incorporate it into a single table—this will serve as your personal Engaged Leader Strategic Plan.

The full worksheet is available at charleneli.com/the-engaged-leader

to an executive—after all, a Millennial may know how to use all the tools yet very little about leadership at the executive level.[48] Instead, start by educating leaders in how digital and social engagement can help them achieve their strategic goals, and then develop tactics on how to learn, share, and engage. Consider using the worksheet shown in Figure 4.5 as part of your digital leadership training.

Conclusion

The framework for becoming an engaged leader—listen, share, engage—will serve as a template for leaders as they undergo their digital transformation and guide others along the journey. All the aspects of the art and science of digital leadership mentioned here are open to anyone. They require only an openness to change, a willingness to practice, and the dedication to prepare by anchoring digital strategy to goals and objectives.

Digital leadership has many benefits, as we've seen, not the least of which is a direct connection to employees, customers, and other important stakeholders. As you move along your journey, always think about your audience—your followers. Using digital to become a more engaged leader can eliminate the divide between you and them and deliver enormous value as a result.

But it takes time because it requires a new and different skill set. As a leader, you are comfortable decoding complicated financial spreadsheets and interpreting analytics. Your job is to multitask: running from airport to airport and toggling with ease among myriad issues and problems. You make big-picture decisions fast and with precision. In doing so, you set the tone for the rest of the organization. Accurate or not, this is the stereotype of the leader—smart, confident, and unabashedly Type A. Yet all this fast action, lone heroism, and grace under pressure seldom acts as a catalyst for becoming an engaged leader.

Rosemary Turner of UPS and Mike Smith of ANZ both admitted that, when it came to seeing the light concerning social and digital tools, their vision came into focus slowly. But when they caught sight of it, the realization was powerful, and it transformed their leadership practices dramatically and for the better. Like Turner and Smith, and many others, allow yourself to proceed moderately as you acclimate to your new surroundings. Success requires an open mind and launching a few trial balloons.

The framework at the center of this book—listen, share, engage—creates a safe runway and grants you permission to practice. Setting aside 10 minutes a day to start, to see what other CEOs are posting on Twitter or what is trending on your company's internal news stream, is enough for week one. You need to take measured steps at first and allow yourself to go through the Kübler-Ross-like stages. This is what will allow you to be your best as an engaged leader. People may be pushing you—your staff, the media, possibly even your kids. Don't take the bait—take your time.

My work with CEOs and executives has proven, time after time, that the wisdom and experience a great leader brings to the table are the keys to making his or her digital transformation stick. Any one of the tens or hundreds of digital natives within your organization can teach you to use Twitter, but only you can know how to use it (and other digital tools and platforms) to make your business better. As a leader you are better than anyone at separating the signals from the noise and analyzing the emerging big picture.

So start slowly, but start now. Becoming an engaged leader and transforming yourself and your organization may be the last thing you want to do at present, but my money says that, in time, you will agree that it is the most important thing on your agenda today. And in time it will transform your agenda, and your business, not just once, but again and again in ways that no one yet knows.

Acknowledgments

This book would not have come to exist if not for an email introduction from my friend and fellow author Kevin Werbach to Shannon Berning and Steve Kobrin at Wharton Digital Press. Thank you, Kevin, for connecting us!

In our first conversation, Shannon asked me a simple question: "What are you passionate about these days?" The answer immediately came to me: seeing leaders transform with digital engagement. Shannon helped me think through the topic, refined it, and believed in it. The result is in your hands.

I also had the substantial help of Jacqueline Murphy, who was my writing partner and collaborator. Jacque and I go *way* back—she was the editor of my first book, *Groundswell*, so there is a fluidity to our discussions. On countless Skype calls, Jacque helped me order my thoughts, pulled out gems, and massaged my words into coherent pages. But more important, I could trust her to tell me when I was going down the wrong path—and also to reassure me that I should heed my inner compass.

The team at Altimeter Group has been and continues to be incredibly supportive. Our COO, Shannon Latta, kept taking things off my plate so I could focus on research and writing, while my longtime assistant, Susan Wu, protected my calendar. Brian Solis made key introductions, and Jon Cifuentes helped develop many of the case studies. I couldn't ask for a more dedicated, stimulating group of people with whom to spend most of my waking hours. #GONG

A special thanks goes to the many leaders in this book who took the time to share their experiences with me. Your stories are an inspiration. I am struck by your generosity, optimism, and responsiveness, and I am envious of the many people in your organization who benefit from your engaged leadership each day.

To my patient husband and children, thank you for leaving me alone so I could write, and intuitively knowing when a hug would sustain me. You carved out precious space in our home amid our remodeling project, helping me move my desk five times in as many months.

Last, thank you to the many, many people I've had the good fortune of connecting and engaging with over the years in real life and on digital channels. Writing a book can be a dark, lonely pursuit, and your questions, comments, and @replies are a constant source not only of ideas, but also of succor and encouragement. Keep it coming!

Notes

1 Press release announcing the partnership between IBM and Twitter, http://www.ibm.com/big-data/us/en/big-data-and-analytics/ibmandtwitter.html, accessed January 2015.

2 Press release announcing the partnership between IBM and Apple, https://www-03.ibm.com/press/us/en/photo/44395.wss. Accessed January 2015.

3 From interviews conducted with IBM Q4 2014.

4 From Gallup's "State of the Global Workplace" report, 2013, http://www.gallup.com/poll/165269/worldwide-employees-engaged-work.aspx. Accessed January 2015.

5 In 2010, Gallup found that 11% of employees were engaged at work, only slightly less than the 13% in 2013. From Gallup's "State of the Global Workplace" report. http://www.gallup.com/poll/165269/worldwide-employees-engaged-work.aspx. Accessed January 2015.

6 From an interview with Chris Laping on June 10, 2014, interviews with Red Robin Q3 2014 and Yammer case study, https://about.yammer.com/customers/red-robin-gourmet-burgers/. Accessed January 2015.

7 From Yammer case study, https://about.yammer.com/customers/red-robin-gourmet-burgers/. Accessed January 2015.

8 From interviews conducted with Telstra Q4 2014 and an interview with David Thodey, January 5, 2015.

9 From an interview with David Thodey, January 5, 2015.

10 From an interview conducted with Maersk Q1 2015 and the blog post at http://maersklinesocial.com/our-social-media-channels-which-one-is-right-for-you/. Accessed January 2015.

11 From interviews conducted with Rosemary Turner on June 30, 2014, and January 15, 2015.

12 From an interview conducted with Rosemary Turner, January 15, 2015.

13 From an interview conducted with Rosemary Turner, January 15, 2015.

14 From an interview conducted with Rosemary Turner, January 15, 2015.

15 Padmasree Warrior's Twitter account is at http://twitter.com/padmasree. Accessed January 2015.

16 See Warrior's post on women in technology at https://www.linkedin.com/ pulse/20140806131850-249790717-redefining-corporate-traditions. Accessed January 2015.

17 An example of Warrior's more personal posts, such as a photo of her painting, is at https://twitter.com/Padmasree/status/553738654179274752. Accessed January 2015.

18 See Warrior's post at https://twitter.com/Padmasree/ status/546390473384787968. Accessed January 2015.

19 Richard Edelman's blog is at http://www.edelman.com/conversations/6-a-m/. Accessed January 2015.

20 Edelman's blog post "Why I Joined My Father's Company" is at http://www. edelman.com/p/6-a-m/why-i-joined-my-fathers-company/, and his post on the 9/11 Museum is at http://www.edelman.com/p/6-a-m/9-11-museum/. Accessed January 2015.

21 Email response from Richard Edelman, January 13, 2015.

22 Roger Martin, "Moving from Strategic Planning to Storytelling," *Harvard Business Review*, June 1, 2010, n.p. Also at https://hbr.org/2010/06/strategies-as-happy-stories/. Accessed January 2015.

23 See John Chamber's duck call video at https://www.youtube.com/ watch?v=CuDnm77wb0M. Accessed January 2015.

24 Email response from Richard Edelman, January 13, 2015.

25 More background on the interactions between Arijit Guha and Mark Bertolini are available at http://abcnews.go.com/Health/aetna-ceo-arizona-student-bond-cancer-diagnosis-broken/story?id=16906861. Accessed January 2015.

26 See Mark Bertolini's tweet at https://twitter.com/mtbert/ status/229014262096490497. Accessed January 2015.

27 See Mark Bertolini's tweet at https://twitter.com/mtbert/ status/229012832967069696. Accessed January 2015.

28 From interviews with Aetna Q1 2015.

29 Geert Hofstede, Gert Jan Hofstede, and Michael Minkov, *Cultures and Organizations: Software of the Mind*, 3rd ed. (McGraw-Hill, 2010).

30 David Thodey's personal engagement with a customer on Twitter can be seen at https://twitter.com/davidthodey/status/545157854286446595. Accessed January 2015.

31 R.E. Kelley, "In Praise of Followers," *Harvard Business Review*, 66 (1988): 142–148. Also at https://hbr.org/1988/11/in-praise-of-followers. Accessed January 2015.

32 Rachel Happe, "The Language of Engagement," *The CR Blog*, The Community Roundtable, http://www.communityroundtable.com/grow/language-engagement/. Accessed January 2015.

33 The post "The Language of Engagement" has a complete list of best practices at http://www.communityroundtable.com/grow/language-engagement/. Accessed January 2015.

34 David Thodey's LinkedIn Influencer posts are available at https://www. linkedin.com/today/author/130682857. The specific comment can be found on Thodey's post at https://www.linkedin.com/pulse/20141020220138-130682857-three-things-i-m-looking-for-when-i-m-the-customer. Accessed January 2015.

35 From an interview with David Thodey, January 5, 2015.

36 From an interview with David Thodey, January 5, 2015.

37 From an interview with David Thodey, January 5, 2015.

38 Barack Obama's "Ask Me Anything" session on Reddit is available at http://www.reddit.com/r/IAmA/comments/z1c9z/i_am_barack_ob. Accessed January 2015.

39 From a discussion with Jeffrey Immelt, March 8, 2010. He was referencing GE CMO Beth Comstock, who is very active on Twitter (http://twitter. com/bethcomstock) and LinkedIn (http://www.linkedin.com/in/ elizabethjcomstock). Accessed January 2015.

40 Read Jeffrey Immelt's tweets at https://twitter.com/jeffimmelt. Accessed January 2015.

41 A transcript of Immelt's Boston College commencement address is available at http://files.gereports.com/wp-content/uploads/2010/05/The-Perfect-Time-to-be-a-Boston-College-Grad.pdf. Accessed January 2015.

42 From an interview with Carolyn Miles on October 31, 2014.

43 Miles's blog is at http://loggingcarolynmiles.savethechildren.org, her columns on *Huffington Post* are at http://www.huffingtonpost.com/carolyn-s-miles, and her Twitter account is https://twitter.com/carolynsave. Accessed January 2015.

44 Example tweet from Carolyn Miles on her trip to Guatemala, https://twitter. com/carolynsave/status/558075865540866048. Accessed January 2015.

45 Smith's LinkedIn posts are available at https://www.linkedin.com/profile/ view?id=275552820. Accessed January 2015.

46 Smith writes about how he became a social media believer in this LinkedIn post: https://www.linkedin.com/pulse/20140414143616-275552820-how-i-became-a-social-media-believer-and-why-banking-s-future-is-digital. Accessed January 2015.

47 From interviews with ANZ's Mike Smith in Q4 2014 and Q1 2015, and Mike Smith's post at https://www.linkedin.com/pulse/20140414143616-275552820-how-i-became-a-social-media-believer-and-why-banking-s-future-is-digital. Accessed January 2015.

48 The Altimeter Group report *Social Media Education for Employees* is available at http://www.altimetergroup.com/2013/12/new-research-how-companies-reduce-social-media-risk-and-activate-employee-advocacy-for-scale. Accessed January 2015.

Index

About the Author

Charlene Li is the founder and CEO of Altimeter Group and the author of the *New York Times* bestseller *Open Leadership: How Social Technology Can Transform How You Lead*. She is also the coauthor of the critically acclaimed, bestselling *Groundswell: Winning in a World Transformed by Social Technologies*, which was named one of the best business books in 2008.

She is one of the foremost experts on digital strategies and a consultant and independent thought leader on leadership, strategy, employee engagement, and marketing. Formerly, Charlene was vice president and principal analyst at Forrester Research, worked in online newspaper publishing, and was a consultant with Monitor Group. She was named one of the 100 most creative people in business by *Fast Company* in 2010 and one of the most influential women in technology in 2009.

Charlene is a much-sought-after public speaker and has keynoted top conferences such as the World Business Forum, World Economic Forum, and SXSW. She is also a trusted adviser to Fortune 500 companies such as Cisco, Southwest Airlines, and UPS.

Charlene is a graduate of Harvard Business School and received a magna cum laude degree from Harvard College. She lives in San Francisco with her husband and two teenagers and regularly indulges in making "slow" foods like sourdough bread to balance her real-time digital life.

Learn More

For more information about Charlene Li
and Altimeter Group, please visit:
http://charleneli.com/the-engaged-leader

For a list of frequently asked questions, visit:
http://charleneli.com/the-engaged-leader/faq

Follow Charlene's work:
http://charleneli.com/blog
http://twitter.com/charleneli
http://linkedin.com/in/charleneli

About Wharton Digital Press

Wharton Digital Press was established to inspire bold, insightful thinking within the global business community. In the tradition of The Wharton School of the University of Pennsylvania and its online business journal, *Knowledge@Wharton*, Wharton Digital Press uses innovative digital technologies to help managers meet the challenges of today and tomorrow.

As an entrepreneurial publisher, Wharton Digital Press delivers relevant, accessible, conceptually sound, and empirically based business knowledge to readers wherever and whenever they need it. Its format ranges from ebooks to Web editions to print books available through print-on-demand technology. Directed to a general business audience, the Press's areas of interest include management and strategy, innovation and entrepreneurship, finance and investment, leadership, marketing, operations, human resources, social responsibility, business-government relations, and more.

http://wdp.wharton.upenn.edu

About The Wharton School

The Wharton School of the University of Pennsylvania—founded in 1881 as the first collegiate business school—is recognized globally for intellectual leadership and ongoing innovation across every major discipline of business education. The most comprehensive source of business knowledge in the world, Wharton bridges research and practice through its broad engagement with the global business community. The School has more than 4,800 undergraduate, MBA, executive MBA, and doctoral students; more than 9,000 annual participants in executive education programs; and an alumni network of 86,000 graduates.

http://wdp.wharton.upenn.edu

CPSIA information can be obtained at www.ICGtesting.com
Printed in the USA
BVOW02s0106040315

390236BV00004B/11/P